Jewish Meditation

A PRACTICAL GUIDE

Aryeh Kaplan

Schocken Books   New York

Copyright © 1985 by Schocken Books Inc.

All rights reserved under International and Pan-American Copyright Conventions. Published in the United States by Schocken Books Inc., New York. Distributed by Pantheon Books, a division of Random House, Inc., New York.

Originally published by Schocken Books in 1985.

Library of Congress Cataloging in Publication Data

Kaplan, Aryeh.
  Jewish meditation.
1. Meditation (Judaism) I. Title.
BM723.K288   1985   296.7′2   84-23589

ISBN 0–8052–4006–3 (hardcover)
      0–8052–0781–3 (paperback)

The publisher acknowledges with gratitude the assistance of Mrs. Anita Lasry in the preparation of this book.

Designed by Cynthia Basil

Manufactured in the United States of America

B987654321

Contents

Introduction

People are often surprised to hear the term "Jewish meditation." Otherwise knowledgeable Jews, including many rabbis and scholars, are not aware that such a thing exists. When shown texts that describe Jewish meditation, they respond that it belongs to esoteric or occult corners of Judaism and has little to do with mainstream Judaism.

It is therefore not surprising that many current books on meditation give scant attention to Judaism. Although most writers seem to be aware that mystical elements exist in Judaism, their discussion is usually restricted to the Kabbalah or the Chasidic masters. Most books on meditation emphasize Eastern practices, and in some instances Christian meditation, but Jewish meditation is for all practical purposes ignored.

For students of meditation, this is a serious oversight. Judaism produced one of the more important systems of meditation, and ignoring it is bound to make any study incomplete. Furthermore, since Judaism is an Eastern religion that migrated to the West, its meditative practices may well be those most relevant to Western man. Without a knowledge of Jewish meditative practices, an important link between East and West is lost. This omission is all the more significant in light of considerable evidence that the Jewish mystical masters had dialogue with the Sufi masters and were also aware of the schools of India.

For the Jew, however, the lacuna is most serious. Jews are by nature a spiritual people, and many Jews actively seek spiritual meaning in life, often on a mystical level. Generations ago, large numbers of Jews were attracted to the mystical traditions of groups such as the Freemasons. Today, many American Jews have become involved in Eastern religions. It is estimated that as many as 75 percent of the devotees in some ashrams are Jewish, and large percentages follow disciplines such as Transcendental Meditation.

When I speak to these Jews and ask them why they are exploring other religions instead of their own, they answer that they know of nothing deep or spiritually satisfying in Judaism. When I tell them there is a strong tradition of meditation and mysticism, not only in Judaism, but in mainstream Judaism, they look at me askance. Until Jews become aware of the spiritual richness of their own tradition, it is understandable that they will search in other pastures.

A few years ago, I was invited to speak in a small synagogue in upstate New York. The weather was bad that evening, and only twenty people showed up, so instead of giving the lecture I had planned, I gathered everyone into a circle and just talked. Most of the people there had relatively little knowledge of Judaism. In the course of our talk, I began to discuss the Shema and how it can be used as a meditation (see chapter 3). One of the women present asked if I would do a demonstration, and I agreed.

The whole meditation could not have taken more than ten or fifteen minutes. Ordinarily, it would have taken longer, but in this situation I felt pressed for time. Still, at the end, everyone present, including me, was literally breathless. Collectively, we had experienced a significant spiritual high.

"Why can't we ever do anything like this at services?" asked one of the men. It was a question I could not answer. The discussion turned to how cold and spiritually sterile synagogue services can be, and how a technique like this, which works so well in a group, could make the service infinitely more meaningful. Together we questioned whether the synagogue service was initially meant to be a meditative experience.

If finding spiritual meaning is difficult for the uncommitted Jew, it is sometimes difficult for the Orthodox Jew as well. I have been approached by yeshiva students who are committed to observing the rituals of Judaism but fail to see how these practices can elevate them spiritually. Even more troubling is the number of Orthodox Jews who are involved in disciplines such as Transcendental Meditation. Most of them express uneasiness about these practices but feel that the benefits outweigh the dangers. When asked why they do not seek this type of experience in Judaism, they give the same answer as uncommitted Jews: they are not aware that such an experience can be found within Judaism.

When my first book on the subject, *Meditation and the Bible*, was published in 1978, it sparked a new interest in Jewish meditation in many circles. For most people, it was the first intimation that Jewish meditation existed. Although the work drew on a considerable amount of published material, most of the sources had never been translated from the Hebrew and were available only to experienced Hebraic scholars. Even then, much of the material was difficult to understand for someone who had not engaged in meditative practices. To make this material accessible, the keys to understanding had to be found, and many of these keys existed only in ancient, unpublished manuscripts.

It is significant that most of the important texts on Jewish meditation have never been published, even in their original Hebrew. The most important works exist only in manuscript, locked away in libraries and museums. To research this book, as well as a subsequent work, *Meditation and Kabbalah*, the manuscripts first had to be located; this involved searching through scholarly journals and library catalogues. Once the manuscripts were found, copies had to be obtained, and when they were located in places like the Lenin Library in Moscow, this was not an easy task. Many of the manuscripts were hundreds of years old, written in obsolete scripts that could be deciphered only with considerable effort. The effort was worth it, however, and many important keys to Jewish meditation were discovered.

Because so little on Jewish meditation was ever published,

many people argued that meditation was to be found only in the backwaters of Judaic literature—in works not even worthy of publication. Actually, many works dealing with Kabbalistic methods of meditation were not published because the practices were dangerous and were not meant for the masses. Still, even these works shed considerable light on obscure passages found in published mainstream works; they are an integral part of the puzzle, without which major areas of Judaism are difficult, if not impossible, to understand. Once the puzzle began to come together, it became clear to me that some of the most important mainstream Jewish leaders of the past relied on various meditative techniques.

With the publication of *Meditation and the Bible,* interest in Jewish meditation began to grow. Even the Lubavitcher Rebbe issued a directive that Jewish forms of meditation should be explored. Groups that taught and practiced Jewish meditation were formed in the United States and Israel. I felt privileged that my books formed the basis of many of these groups.

Unfortunately, a number of groups also involved in "Jewish meditation" were practicing something far from Judaism. Some of them attempted to adapt Eastern practices to Jewish audiences, or to Judaize Eastern teachings. Although these groups attracted a following of sorts, they were not teaching Jewish meditation.

Meanwhile, together with a group of committed Jewish psychiatrists and psychologists, I began to experiment with the techniques I had found in the literature. Together we explored the inner space of the meditative state. Among the participants were David Sheinkin (of blessed memory), Seymour Applebaum, and Paul (Pinchas) Bindler. Other members who made important contributions to the group were Arnie and Roz Gellman, Miriam Benhaim Circlin, Sylvia Katz, Jeff Goldberg, Gerald Epstein, Perle Epstein, and many others.

One important discovery we made was that most texts dealing with Jewish meditation assume that the reader is familiar with the general techniques, and intend only to provide additional detail. The details were fascinating, but when we tried to translate them into practice, we discovered that too much information was missing. It was like trying to use a book on advanced French cuisine without a rudimentary knowledge of cooking. The recipes were there, but a novice could not use them. In the case of Jewish meditation, the ingredients were there, but the means of mixing them together were omitted or glossed over.

To some degree, the puzzle was pieced together in my two previous meditation books. However, neither of these books was meant to be a practical guide. Many people expressed the need for a guide to Jewish meditation written in nontechnical terms for the layperson. It was out of these requests that the idea for this book was born.

This book presents the most basic forms of Jewish meditation, especially as discussed in mainstream sources. It assumes no special background on the part of the reader either in Judaism or in meditation. It is my hope that this book will at least begin to provide its readers with insight into the spiritual dimensions of the Jewish heritage.

Aryeh Kaplan
December 17, 1982

Jewish
Meditation

1·What Is Meditation?

What is meditation? For someone who has been involved in the practice, the question need not be asked. For a person who has never had any contact with meditation, however, the subject is shrouded in mystery. To many people, the term "meditation" suggests an image of someone sitting in the lotus position with eyes closed in serene concentration. Others may associate meditation with holiness and spirituality. Individuals seeking spirituality might look into various disciplines of meditation without having any idea of what they are looking for.

In its most general sense, meditation consists of thinking in a controlled manner. It is deciding exactly how one wishes to direct the mind for a period of time, and then doing it.

In theory this may sound very easy, but in practice it is not. The human mind is not a domesticated animal, but rather seems to have a mind of its own beyond the will of the thinker. Anyone who has ever tried to concentrate on a subject, only to have his mind drift to other thoughts, is aware of this. Sometimes it seems that the more one tries to control one's thoughts, the more they refuse to be controlled.

It is strange that most people have never given a thought to their thoughts. Thoughts are so much part of our being that we take them for granted. One of the first steps in meditation is learning how not to take our thoughts for granted.

A simple exercise will demonstrate how difficult it is to control your thoughts. In theory this exercise seems ridiculously simple, but in practice it is tantalizingly difficult.

This is the exercise: Stop thinking.

Normally, when one is not otherwise occupied, there is a constant flow of thought passing through the mind. In this reverie, one thought flows into another, almost automatically. This flow of thought goes on and on, like an internal conversation with oneself. Usually, this reverie is so much part of our mental environment that we do not pay attention to it.

The first exercise is to become aware of your thoughts by trying to stop them. Try to blank out your mind for a few minutes and not think of anything at all. Sound easy? Stop reading now and try it.

All right. How long did it last? Unless you are very unusual, or have had meditative experience, you could not keep your mind blank for more than a few seconds. If nothing more, the period of mental silence was probably interrupted by the thought, "I'm not thinking," or "I'm trying not to think." In practice, it is extremely difficult to turn off thought. As we shall see, control over the thought process is one of the goals of some meditative disciplines.

There is another way in which you can try to control your mind. When you finish this paragraph, close your eyes. You will probably see lights or images flashing before your eyes. Give yourself a few moments to relax, and these flashing lights will subside and develop into a series of kaleidoscopic images in the mind's eye. These images will arise and change spontaneously with little or no direction by the conscious mind. One image flows into another as still another grows and develops. It is almost impossible to concentrate on these mind-begotten images, because when you try, they disappear.

Now, with your eyes closed, try to control these images. Try to depict the letter *A* in your mind's eye. Unless you have practiced this technique for some time, it is impossible to hold on to this image.

One of the techniques of meditation is "imaging," evoking an image in the mind's eye and holding it there. In Jewish meditation, this is known as "engraving." Here the image is fixed in the mind as if it were engraved, so that it can be held in the mind as long as one desires. This technique can be perfected only through extensive training.

Having tried these two exercises, you can see that the mind has a "mind of its own." There are thus two parts to the mind, one that is under the control of the conscious will and one that is not. That part of the mind under the control of the will is called the consciousness, while that which is not is called the unconscious or subconscious. Since the subconscious is not under the control of the will, one cannot control what it passes into the conscious mind.

One of the goals of meditation, then, is to gain control of the subconscious part of the mind. If one were to succeed, one would also gain a high degree of self-mastery. This, too, is a goal of meditation.

This explains why so many disciplines use breathing exercises as a meditative device. Breathing usually occurs automatically and is therefore normally under the control of the unconscious mind. Unless you are consciously controlling your breathing, it will mirror your unconscious mood. This is one reason why breathing is one of the indicators in a lie detector test.

Yet, if you wish, you can control your breath, and do so quite easily. Breathing therefore forms a link between the conscious mind and the unconscious. By learning how to concentrate on and control your breath you can go on to learn how to control the unconscious mind.

The thought process itself is also controlled to a large degree by the unconscious, but it can also be controlled by the conscious mind. This is most obvious in the case of the reverie. When one is relaxing and not paying particular attention to it, the reverie flows from one thought to another without conscious effort. Indeed, there are a number of psychological techniques that try to imitate this "free association," in order to gain an understanding of the unconscious mind. However, no matter how free the association may be when one is expressing it to a second party, it is never as free as in the case of pure reverie. The reverie thus can also be seen as a point of interface between the conscious and unconscious. By learning how to control the reverie, one can also learn how to control the unconscious.

The same is true of the visions that appear in the mind's eye. Since they are not under the control of the conscious mind, they are obviously coming from the unconscious. Controlling them is very difficult without practice; one can learn to control them, however, and doing so also serves to form a bridge between the conscious mind and the unconscious.

One of the most powerful benefits of meditation is control over the unconscious mind. One learns to use the conscious mind to control mental processes that are usually under the control of the unconscious. Gradually, more and more of the subconscious becomes accessible to the conscious mind, and one gains control of the entire thought process.

Sometimes, different parts of the mind appear to be acting independently. The conflict between two parts of the mind can be so strong that a person feels like two separate individuals. During such inner conflict, it seems that one part of the mind wants to do one thing, while the other part wants to do something else.

Thus, for example, a person may be drawn toward a sexual temptation. One part of the mind is thus saying yes very loudly. Yet, at the same time, another part of the mind may feel that the act is morally reprehensible. This second part of the mind may be saying no with equal loudness. The person may feel caught in the middle, between the two voices.

In classical Freudian psychology, this would be seen as a conflict between the id and the superego. In our example, the id would be saying yes to the temptation, while the superego would be saying no. Somehow, the ego (the "I") mediates between these two subconscious voices. Although Freud's schema ties it into a neat package, introspection shows that the conflict is actually more complex than the simple picture of the id and superego. Sometimes not two but three, four, or more voices seem to be giving different signals in the mind. If a person were to learn to control his subconscious, he could avoid much of this conflict.

There are many theories about the subconscious, and a full discussion is far beyond the scope of this book. However, if meditation is controlled thinking, it implies that the individual has the entire thought process under control, including input from the subconscious. The experienced meditator learns how to think what he wants to think, when he wants to think it. He can always be in control of the situation, resisting psychological pressures that work on the subconscious. He is also in control of himself, never doing something that he knows he really does not want to do. In many schools, this self-mastery is one of the most important goals of meditation.

2 · Why Meditate?

Meditation, which is thought directed by will, can bring many benefits. Most people learn how to think as very young children, and throughout their adult lives, they do not think any differently than they did as children. That is to say, most people use their minds in a manner not essentially different from the way they did when they were six years old. Through meditation, one can control the thought process and learn to think in new ways, thus gaining new and richer mind experiences.

It is significant that in Kabbalah, one's normal mode of thinking is referred to as the "mentality of childhood" (*mochin de-katnuth*). More advanced modes of thought and states of consciousness, on the other hand, are referred to as the "mentality of adulthood" (*mochin de-gadluth*). One learns these methods of "adult thought" through meditation, through which one develops the ability to transcend the ways of thinking one learned as a child.

In chapter 1, for example, we discussed how different parts of the mind act independently. Thus, a person might want to concentrate on a task at hand, but at the same time other concerns pop into his mind, disturbing his concentration. While one part of the mind is trying to focus on a problem, other parts may be drawing attention to different ideas. As long as this is true, concentration is not complete.

For this reason, a person usually uses only a small portion of the mind. As much as he might try to concentrate on a thought or task, parts of his mind are engaged in other activities. Sometimes the rest of the mind is merely passive. At other times however, other parts of the mind may actually be acting in opposition to one's concentration. Unless one is able to control the entire mind, one cannot develop full concentration.

People often think of concentration in terms of problem-solving. It can also involve the most basic of experiences. Suppose, for example, that you are trying to experience the beauty of a rose. At the same time, thoughts about your business may be pushing their way into your mind. Your attention does not stay focused on the rose and you cannot see the rose totally, in all its beauty.

But there is another factor that prevents you from experiencing the rose completely. Earlier, we discussed the spontaneous images that arise in the field of vision when the eyes are closed. Actually, you can also see these images with your eyes open in a darkened room. Once you are aware of these images, you can even see them with your eyes open in a well-lit room. The reason you are normally not aware of these images is that they are very faint compared with the images entering your mind from your open eyes. Nevertheless, they are constantly with you.

Now suppose you are trying to appreciate the beauty of a rose. No matter how hard you try to focus your mind on the rose, the image of the rose is competing with the self-generated images in the mind. It is as if there were a screen of extraneous imagery between you and the rose, preventing you from seeing it with total clarity.

In a meditative state, however, it is possible to turn off the interference and concentrate totally on the rose. As we shall see, with training, one can turn off the spontaneous self-generated images and thus remove the screen. The beauty of the flower when seen in these higher states of awareness is indescribable to someone who has never experienced it. The most I can say is that the rose actually appears to radiate beauty. This can be true of anything else in the world.

Another important goal of meditation is thus enhanced awareness and perception. The greater the portion of the mind focused on an experience, the more the experience will be enhanced. When every cell in your brain is tuned in to experiencing the rose, the experience is indescribably different from what you would see in your usual state of consciousness.

This works in one of two ways. The most simple way in which meditation works is to quiet down all parts of the mind not concentrating on the immediate experience. In this mode, the experience is not enhanced directly, but rather all interference with it is removed. Thus, you may be looking at the rose with no greater awareness than before, but without the mental static, it will appear much more vivid. It is somewhat like trying to tune in to a faint radio station; even if you cannot amplify the volume, you will hear the station more clearly if you can eliminate the static. This mode of meditation can be reached through most meditative techniques and is the state of consciousness most readily attainable in its lower levels.

The second way in which meditation can enhance an experience is by focusing more of the mind on it. Ultimately, as one becomes a more experienced meditator, one can learn to focus the entire mind on a single experience. This is analogous to turning up the volume of a radio or using a system of greater fidelity. This level is attained in the more advanced states of meditation, and one can use it to exert the total force of one's mind on anything one desires.

Of course, neither mode is generally attained without the other. When you quiet other areas of the mind, you also focus more of the mind on the experience. Conversely, focusing more of the mind on the experience almost always involves blocking out other experiences and thoughts.

This increased awareness can be used in many ways. Meditation can be used to gain a greater and clearer awareness of the world around us. Looking at something like a rose while in a meditative state of consciousness, one can see much more in it than one would otherwise see. It has been said that one can see the entire universe in a grain of sand. In a high meditative state, this is actually possible. As one's capacity for concentration increases, one can also become aware of subtle phenomena that are not otherwise detectable. Thus, the world of the meditator may become much richer than that of those who have never had the experience.

Here again, there is a language barrier. If one has never experienced these phenomena, then one cannot comprehend a description of them. The situation can be better understood through analogy.

For the average sighted person, a page of braille feels like bumpy paper and nothing more. A blind person, however, does not have his sense of sight competing with his sense of touch, and hence experiences less "static." Furthermore, since he uses his sense of touch more often, his tactile sense is enhanced. With practice, he learns to decipher the patterns of raised dots as letters and words. It is true that a sighted person can also learn to read braille, but those who have mastered it usually read with their eyes closed, so that their faculty of sight will not interfere with their sense of touch.

Reading braille is a good example of an experience that is meaningless to a nonsensitized person but has a world of meaning for a sensitized person. Many such experiences may exist in the world, and meditation can teach one to "read" these messages.

Another analogy may express this even more clearly. Many blind people learn to navigate by listening to the subliminal echoes given off by buildings and other large objects. This is why blind people often tap their canes constantly; they listen to the echoes produced by the tapping, and the echoes warn them of obstructions. The strange thing is that blind people claim that they do not actually hear these echoes, but sense them in a manner that they cannot describe. Rather than speak of this experience as hearing an echo, a blind person will describe it as sensing an obstruction. These echoes are not perceptible to a sighted person since the flood of information experienced through vision overwhelms them completely. Moreover, there is a learning period during which a blind person becomes sensitized to these echoes.

On a more esoteric level, in Tibetan medicine, as well as in Kabbalah, a number of illnesses can be diagnosed merely by feeling the pulse. The subtle differences in the feel and rhythm of the pulse can provide a skilled practitioner with a picture of the body's state of health with uncanny accuracy. Observing the Dalai Lama's personal physician make such a diagnosis, a famous doctor reported that he had witnessed something bordering on the supernatural.

The secret, however, is twofold. First, the practitioner must learn to enter a deep state of concentration in which the pulse beat fills his entire world of sensation and the subtlest variations in it stand out clearly and vividly. The practitioner is thus able to garner a great deal of information from the pulse beat. To him, every pulse beat is an encyclopedia of information about the body. Once he learns how to "read" the pulse beat in this manner, he can then learn what every variation means. People who have attempted to learn this technique report that it can take as much as fifteen years to master it well enough to make an accurate diagnosis.

A number of Judaic sources speak of meditation as a means of attaining extrasensory perception (ESP) in such areas as telepathy, mind-reading, clairvoyance, and predicting the future. These powers may also involve increased awareness. In the ordinary state of consciousness, ESP signals received by the mind may be overshadowed by the perceptual information entering the brain, as well as by the mind's natural "static" or "noise." As discussed earlier, this static consists of thoughts and images spontaneously produced by the mind which are not under the conscious mind's control. In the meditative state, when this noise or static is quieted, ESP phenomena may become more readily discernible. A number of ESP experiments appear to indicate that this is true, and that meditation enhances the effect. Unfortunately, as in the case of most ESP experiments, results depend on so many variables that unambiguous conclusions are difficult to obtain.

Another purpose of meditation is to attune the mind to certain truths (or Truths with a capital *T*). When a person tries to explore questions such as the meaning of existence, the true goal of life, or the ultimate nature of reality, the answers remain elusive, tickling the edge of the mind. Possible answers hover on the borderline of consciousness, but are so subtle that they cannot be discerned through the static of the mind.

One of the most elusive truths is knowledge of the self. Generally we see ourselves only through a thick veil of ego. For this reason, it is impossible to see ourselves as others see us. Through meditation, however, we can remove the veil of ego, and see ourselves with a degree of objectivity. In this manner, we can look at ourselves objectively as a third person. We are then able to see our own shortcomings and overcome them.

The self-awareness engendered by meditation can also strengthen the ego when needed. Thus, a person with a weak self-image and feelings of inadequacy can learn to be more self-assured. He can examine his motivations and learn to become more inner-directed, doing the things he desires, and not simply what others expect of him. He can look objectively at his relationships with others and learn to improve them.

One of the most powerful uses of meditation is to gain an awareness of the spiritual. Although we may be surrounded by a sea of spirituality, we are not usually aware of it. Spiritual sensations are quite faint and usually overshadowed by the world of the senses. Even in a state of sensory deprivation, the self-generated thoughts of the mind tend to obscure spiritual sensation. However, if a person can quiet down all extraneous thoughts, he can then "tune in" to the spiritual. This tuning-in is what is known as the mystical experience. In this sense, meditation is the most important technique of mystics all over the world.

The most vivid experiences were those attained by the prophets in the Bible. In the biblical sense, a prophet is more than a person who merely sees the future. Rather, he is one who has such a strong experience of the spiritual that he can use it to garner information. Sometimes this information includes knowledge of the future, hence the popular conception of a prophet as one who sees what has not yet occurred. Nevertheless, the true prophet has access to many other truths besides knowledge of the future. It is important to realize the important role that meditation played in the careers of the prophets of Israel.

On its highest level, meditation can provide a person with an experience of God. This is certainly the highest possible spiritual experience. Our perception of God is often clouded by ego and anthropomorphism, so that we tend to see God as a mirror image of ourselves. By freeing the mind of these encumbrances, meditation can help us to open our minds totally to the experience of God. In many religious traditions, including Judaism, this is the highest goal of meditation.

3 · Techniques

At this point it would be useful to discuss and classify the various meditative techniques, both Jewish and non-Jewish. The techniques of almost all meditative systems can be classified in similar ways; this does not imply any special relationship between Jewish and non-Jewish meditation. Rather, since a general concept of meditation exists, all forms have characteristics in common, which in turn can be used to classify various techniques.

The situation is analogous to that of prayer, which is important in all religious traditions. Certain elements are characteristic of all prayer. This does not mean that one system of prayer is derived from another, or even that a relationship exists between the systems. Rather, the similarities stem from the fact that there are a limited number of basic ways of relating to God, and these will be found in prayer wherever it exists.

Thus, almost every prayer can fit into one of three categories: praise, petition, and thanksgiving. We can praise God and speak of His greatness. We can petition God and ask Him to provide us with the things we need and want. Finally, we can thank God for what He has given us. In Jewish prayer, these three divisions are formalized and follow a set sequence. Nevertheless, if we were to examine prayers of all the world's faiths, we would find that with few exceptions they would all fall into one of the three categories.

The same is true of meditation. There are a finite number of ways in which a person can interact with his own mind, and these form the categories of all meditation. Thus, when one understands meditation in general, one can then understand Jewish meditation in particular. Since meditation involves subtle experiences that may be unfamiliar to many readers, I shall begin with a mundane example.

I have defined meditation as a controlled manner of thinking. On the simplest level, you can decide to sit down for the next half hour and just think about one particular subject. Let's say you decide that for the next half hour you will think about rearranging your furniture. In your mind's eye, you might imagine how various arrangements would look and even plan how to move the heavier pieces. During that half hour, you will have been meditating on furniture arrangement. It is as simple as that. There need not be anything esoteric or mysterious about meditation. No special surroundings are required, nor must any particular body position be assumed. You could have meditated while walking around the block, while sitting back in your easy chair, or while relaxing in the tub. The very fact that for a specific time period you were thinking about a specific topic rather than letting your mind wander at random makes it a meditative experience.

Of course, it is not always that easy. What do you do when other thoughts begin to creep into the mind? Remember that the decision was to think about arranging furniture *and nothing else*. If this meditation is actually going to be a controlled thinking experience, then you will need a technique to rid yourself of undesired thoughts. You might gently push the extraneous thoughts out of your mind or otherwise pull your mind back to the desired subject. Whatever method you use to keep your mind on the subject, in doing so you will be developing the rudiments of a full-fledged meditative technique.

Meditation on rearranging your furniture may be a trivial example. But suppose you decided to spend a half hour meditating on how to rearrange your life. You might find yourself thinking about fundamental questions such as these:

What do I ultimately want out of life?
What gives my life meaning?
What is the meaning of life in general?
If I had my life to live over, what would I do with it?
What ideals, if any, would I be willing to die for?
What would bring me more happiness than anything else in
   the world?

You have probably already thought about these questions at some time in your life. However, chances are that you thought of them only briefly. Unless you have been involved in a discipline that encourages it, you have probably never spent a full half hour, without interruption, thinking about any of these questions. If you have never done so before, the first time may be very shocking. You may discover that you have no idea of what you perceive as your purpose in life. You may have never thought about the meaning of life at all.

Indeed, after a half hour of pondering any of the above questions, you might decide that the question needs more than one session of meditation. You might decide to have a half-hour session once a week. To make sure that you continue, you may decide that at a certain time every week you will spend a half hour meditating on the purpose of life as well as your own personal goals. You will then be on your way to developing a discipline of meditation.

After several weeks of such meditation, you will probably begin to notice yourself growing in a number of areas. You might decide to reevaluate the direction of your life and make major changes in your life-style. You might find yourself more secure in your dealings with others, more confident about how you are spending your time. You may also find that you are constantly gaining new insight into your own personality and motivations.

At this point, you might feel that once a week is not enough. You may decide to increase the frequency of your meditation to two or three times a week or even once a day. You will then discover why many schools of meditation suggest or require that meditation be a daily exercise.

As you continue to explore what is most meaningful to you, you may come to a point where you feel that you are reaching a new threshold. You may find yourself pondering not only the meaning of your own life, but the very meaning of existence in general.

At this point, you will have discovered God.

Before discussing this further, it is important to define God. We often think of God as being "out there," far away from the world. But it is important to realize that God is also "in there"— in the deepest recesses of the soul.

Here are two ways in which a person can discover God.

First, a person can reflect on questions such as these: What is beyond space and time? How did the world come into existence? Why does the world exist? What came before time? By pondering such questions, a person can find God, but he will find God only in the sense that God is "out there."

The second way in which one can find God is by delving deeper and deeper into the self in the manner discussed earlier. Here also one finds God, but one is finding Him in the sense that He is "in there."

This twofold manner of discovering God is related to the Kabbalistic concept that God both encompasses and fills all creation. When we say that God is above all things and beyond all things, we are speaking of Him in the sense that He encompasses and defines all creation. This is the concept of God as being "out there." However, in another sense, God is very close to us— closer than the air we breathe, closer than our very souls—and in this sense He fills all creation, and is "in there."

Once a person discovers God in this manner, he might want to transform his meditation into a conversation with God. If one discovers God as the ultimate depth of one's being, then the way to relate to this depth would be to relate to God. At this point, one's meditation into the meaning of existence might become a silent conversation with God.

It is significant to note that according to the Midrash, this is exactly how Abraham's career began. First Abraham began to contemplate the meaning of life and existence, and it was in this manner that he discovered God. Abraham then began to have a dialogue with God. Abraham's experience can be seen as a paradigm of how to begin a relationship with the Divine.

Again, the problem of extraneous thoughts may arise. One way to help alleviate this problem is to speak to God out loud rather than just in the mind. One would then be speaking to God orally.

Using oral conversation as a meditative technique is an ancient Jewish practice, documented in a number of important texts. In particular, it was a technique stressed by Rabbi Nachman of Bratslav, as we shall see in chapter 10.

There are three important things that could be said about the above type of meditation:

1. It is a verbal type of meditation: it involves words in thought or speech, rather than images.
2. It is inner-directed: the entire form of the meditation comes from within the person rather than being determined by an external stimulus.
3. It is unstructured: when the person sits down to meditate, he has no preconceived notion of what direction the meditation will take.

Some people find an unstructured meditation too loose. In order to put structure into your meditation, you can write out an agenda. You may decide that every day for a given period of time, say a week, you will meditate on one subject; then you will go on to a second subject for the next week. Thus, if you are meditating on how to reorder your life, you might decide to spend one week meditating on your relationship with your spouse, a second week meditating on your relationship with your children, and then two weeks meditating on your career.

As soon as one sets up an agenda of meditation, it becomes a structured meditation. Of course, a meditation can be loosely structured or tightly structured, again depending on what one wishes to accomplish. Meditating with an agenda is a practice favored by the Musar schools in Judaism. This form of meditation is especially effective when one wants to perfect one's habits or one's way of life in general.

Another way to add structure to your meditation is to use a biblical verse as the object of meditation. You could take verses randomly from the Bible or seek out verses that apply to the subject of your meditative interest. It is possible to make the entire meditative session, for a day, a week, or a month, revolve around that verse. Your goal would still be to rearrange your life, but you would be trying to do so in the context of that biblical verse. The verse could also form the basis of a conversation with God.

The method of basing a meditation on a verse, known as *gerushin*, was used by the mystics of Safed in the sixteenth century. Although the method was used extensively, the texts provide few details. It appears that a number of ways are possible.

The simplest way to use a biblical verse as a meditation would be to read the verse before meditating, perhaps memorizing it, and then use it as a point of departure for unstructured meditation. The meditator begins by meditating on the verse and then goes on to direct his mind to the subject upon which he wants to meditate. The course of meditation could lead the meditator far from the original verse; the verse would serve merely as the initial focus of the meditation, not as its entire subject. This means of meditation is also discussed in Judaic literature.

Alternatively, you may write the verse on a piece of paper. During the course of meditation, you could then reread it, directing your mind back to the verse from time to time. This is particularly effective if you wish to apply the verse to a particular life problem; in this way, the verse becomes an integral part of the meditation.

Eventually, you may wish to make the verse the entire subject of meditation. In a sense, your meditation would become a conversation with the biblical verse. You would be thinking about the verse, looking at it in different ways, seeking different possible interpretations, and attempting to apply it to your particular life problems. If the verse has a specific lesson, you might use a series of meditative sessions to integrate the verse into your personality. Although we have used a biblical verse as an example, any saying or teaching could be used as the basis for such

a meditation. To simplify our discussion, however, we will continue to speak of a biblical verse.

The verse can be used either visually or verbally.

If the verse is used visually as the basis for meditation, write
the verse on a piece of paper and use it as a focus. Fix your gaze
on the verse; do not take your eyes off it. The verse should
become the center of your attention to the exclusion of everything else. It should be as if nothing else in the world exists other
than the verse. You can then gaze at the verse and allow your
thoughts to flow freely. On a more advanced level, you could use
this method to clear the mind of all thought other than the verse.

This method is known as visual contemplation. Using a verse is
just one means of accomplishing such meditation. The subject of
your contemplation could also be a candle flame, a flower, a
picture, a pebble, or any other object.

Since this practice entails using something external to the
mind as the object of meditation, it is known as an externally
directed meditation. This meditation can be either structured or
unstructured.

The simplest way to do the meditation would be to gaze at the
object and let your thoughts flow freely. This would be an unstructured meditation. However, if you used the method to fill
the mind completely, banishing all other thoughts, then this in
itself would impose structure on the meditation, and it would
constitute a structured meditation.

When one contemplates an object, one looks at it, paying acute
attention to every detail. As one continues to gaze, even the most
minute details become significant. One can look deeper and
deeper into the object, trying to see its inner essence and obliter-
ating all other thought from the mind. Beyond the inner essence,
one can strive to see the Divine in the object and use it as a
springboard to reach God.

In lieu of gazing at the written verse, you could repeat the
verse over and over for the entire period of meditation. This
would be a verbal meditation as opposed to a visual contemplation. Here again, the meditation could be unstructured, where
the mind is allowed to roam wherever the verse takes it. Alterna-

tively, it could be structured, where all thought other than the words of the verse is removed from the mind.

Of course, here again, the subject of meditation need not be a biblical verse. Any sentence, word, or phrase can do. As we shall see, the great Chasidic leader Rabbi Nachman of Bratslav prescribed using the phrase "Lord of the Universe" as a meditative device.

In Eastern traditions, the repeated phrase is known as a mantra, and meditation using such a phrase is called mantra meditation. One of the best-known examples of a system based on mantra meditation is Transcendental Meditation. Since there is no equivalent English term for this type of meditation, I shall use the term "mantra" where necessary.

There are, then, three ways in which the above-mentioned meditations can be classified. They can be either visual or verbal, structured or unstructured, internally or externally directed.

Inner-directed, unstructured meditation is most valuable as a means of examining one's life or finding meaning in life. Externally directed, structured meditation is most often used to focus the mind and thought processes or to gain a transcendental experience.

Although most meditative methods are visual or verbal, other faculties can be the focus of meditation as well. Thus, instead of meditating on an object or verse, one could meditate on a sound, such as the chirping of a cricket, the rush of a waterfall, or a musical note played over and over. One would be using the sense of hearing to direct the meditation, although in these cases the meditation would be nonverbal.

In a similar manner, the meditation could involve the sense of smell. Indeed, there are Hebrew blessings said over fragrances, and in practice they can make the enjoyment of a fragrance into a meditative experience. The blessings over food can make a meditative experience out of tasting and eating. The sense of touch, too, can be the focus of a meditative experience.

It is also possible to use the kinesthetic sense as the object of meditation. This would consist of meditating on a body movement or a series of body movements. This is a method used by the Sufis in their dance meditations. Chasidim often use this form of meditation in dancing and in their slow swaying motions.

Any action meditation can be seen as using the kinesthetic sense, even if other senses are involved. The main thing is to concentrate on the act and elevate it to an expression of divine worship. This can include even mundane acts such as washing the dishes.

In Judaism, action meditation is most important when connected with the performance of the commandments and rituals. Many Jews and non-Jews think of the precepts as routine, ritualistic actions. Many Jewish sources, however, speak of the commandments as meditative devices, which can bring a person to a high level of God consciousness. When the commandments are seen in this light, they assume great spiritual significance.

A final focus of meditation can be one's own emotions. Thus, for example, one can focus on the emotion of love in exactly the same way that one can focus on a flower or a candle flame. One can ponder the love one feels for another person and enhance the emotion, experiencing it totally without any outside interference. One can also take this intensified love and direct it toward God or toward one's fellow man. Indeed, the commandments "Love God your Lord with all your heart, all your soul, and all your might" (Deut. 6:5) and "Love your neighbor like yourself" (Lev. 19:18) actually mandate such a meditation. When one directs one's mind to love God and one's fellow man, one provides one's life with an entirely new focus.

Control of the emotions is a very important element of self-control in general. Often the concept of self-control conjures up the image of an emotionless, dry, rigid way of life. If a person is in complete control of his emotions, however, he can call forth any emotion he desires and is free to enhance it as he wills. Rather than be controlled by emotions such as love, yearning, or awe, he can control them. One can evoke these emotions and blend them together, painting every aspect of life with a rich palette of feelings. Control of the emotions can thus lead a person to experience a richer blend of feelings in his daily life than the average person generally experiences.

The final types of meditation do not make use of any device, but involve direct control of the thoughts. These are usually considered the most advanced forms of meditation.

One such technique involves the exercise mentioned in chapter 1, in which you were asked to try to stop thinking for a period of time. For most people this is impossible, and it is an excellent demonstration that the mind is not entirely under the control of the will. After a few seconds of trying not to think, thoughts begin to creep into the mind, and after a short period, they often return in a torrent.

Like many other disciplines, this, too, can be developed. If a person practices stopping his thought flow, he can learn to do so for longer and longer periods; eventually, he can learn to turn his thought processes on and off at will. This may sound easy, but in practice it takes years of intense practice to perfect this ability.

Since this type of meditation does not use anything as a focus, it is often called nondirected meditation. In its more advanced forms, it can actually focus on "nonthought" or on nothingness. This form of meditation can be dangerous and should not be attempted without a practiced guide or master.

Most of the methods that I shall discuss in this book, however, are fairly straightforward and safe if practiced properly. They can be readily learned and can bring the meditator to increased awareness and higher states of consciousness.

4·States of Consciousness

Most discussions of meditation speak of higher states of consciousness that can be attained through the practice. For the initiate these states of consciousness may be familiar, but for the outsider they are extremely difficult even to imagine. Much has been written about higher states of consciousness, but the discussion usually concludes with a statement that these states are indescribable and ineffable.

There is an important reason that such experiences are indescribable. In the case of objective, external phenomena, a group of people can agree on words to describe them. This is how language in general is constructed. Thus, two people can look at a rose and agree that it is red. Since they are both seeing the same rose, they both have a common experience of which they can speak.

However, when people try to discuss personal experiences in higher states of consciousness, the experiences are entirely internal. I have no way of knowing what is in your mind, so even if you try to describe it, I have no way of being sure of what you mean. Furthermore, since the experiences are internal and individual, it is difficult for people to find a common ground to develop a descriptive vocabulary. Vocabulary is based on shared experiences, and by definition, internal experiences are difficult if not impossible to share.

For example, let us assume that while in a meditative state, I saw in my mind a color that has no counterpart in the external world. Suppose it was totally different from any other color and impossible to describe in terms of other colors. How could I even begin to describe what the color looked like? There would be no words in human vocabulary to describe it. The same is true of many meditative experiences. This fact makes it extremely difficult to develop an epistemology of the meditative state. One ends up trying to describe experiences for which no language exists.

This may be true, but since one of the aims of meditation is to reach higher states of consciousness, we should at least have some idea what this means. The problem is that higher states of consciousness are not only difficult to describe, but also difficult to define. There appears to be no objective epistemology through which one can know for sure that one is in a state of consciousness different from the everyday waking state. Nevertheless, on the basis of subjective experiences and reports, it is possible to gain some understanding of these states of consiousness.

The two most familiar states of consciousness are the waking state and the sleeping state. These are two states of consciousness that are universally known and recognized.

Beyond that, we know that sometimes we may feel drowsy, while at other times we are particularly alert. This demonstrates that there are different levels in the waking state of consciousness. Experiments in which brain waves are measured also indicate that different states of brain activity exist in the waking state. Evidence from sleep laboratories indicates that there are also at least two states of consciousness involved in sleep, the first being the nondream state and the second being the dream state, in which rapid eye movement (REM) is observed.

Certain drugs have an effect on a person's state of consciousness. The best known is alcohol, which has the general effect of diminishing alertness, although since it removes inhibitions, it can also lead to increased awareness in some areas. Other, more potent drugs, such as LSD and mescaline, appear to increase the ability to focus on specific sensations, such as beauty, color, form, and the like. A full discussion of drug-induced states of consciousness is beyond the scope of this book. Instead, we shall explore states of consciousness that can be self-induced.

I recall that when I was in *yeshivah,* a few friends and I decided to have a contest to see who could memorize the most pages of Talmud. For me, it was an interesting experience. The first page took considerable effort and time, perhaps several hours. As I continued, each page became progressively easier. Eventually, after ten pages or so, I found that I could memorize a page after three or four readings. By the time I had gone through some twenty pages, I could memorize a page with a single reading. What had originally been extremely difficult had become relatively easy. My friends reported the same experience.

It is well known that memory is a faculty that can be trained. People who regularly memorize large quantities of information find themselves able to do so very readily. Professional actors, for example, can memorize the lines in a play or movie in one or two readings. Similarly, many professional musicians can memorize a score almost immediately.

What was interesting from a subjective viewpoint was that it did not seem to me that my memory had improved. Rather, it seemed that when I looked at a page, I was looking at it differently. It was as if my memory was wide open and the material was going directly into it. It felt as if there was normally a barrier between perception and memory and that this barrier had now been removed.

Logically, this would make sense. If we remembered everything we saw or learned, our memory would rapidly become cluttered with useless information. The mind therefore has a sort of filter that prevents unwanted information from being stored in the memory. The problem is that the filter is sometimes there when one does not want it—such as when one wishes to memorize something. With training, however, one can learn to remove this filter at will.

The point is that when a person has trained his mind to memorize, his awareness when reading material to be memorized is completely different. It could be said that he is in a different state of consciousness at the time.

Let me give another example. When I was a graduate student in nuclear physics, I was once working on an extremely difficult mathematical problem for a paper. I became totally involved in the problem and worked on it for almost seventy-two hours without interruption. In order to solve the problem, I had to invent a number of original mathematical techniques and procedures. But the strange thing was that when I read the final paper two years later, I found it almost impossible to understand the mathematics. It was difficult to believe that I had created this mathematical structure.

Anyone who has ever worked on a difficult problem, especially in mathematics or the sciences, knows that at a certain point the mind seems to "lock on" to the problem. At that point, solving the problem becomes the most important thing in the world, and every fiber of one's being is concentrated on finding a solution. Subjectively speaking, I know that I can accomplish things when in a "locked-on" state that I cannot accomplish otherwise.

In one of my advanced physics courses, I had a difficult mathematical problem on a test. I worked on the problem for a while and then, realizing that I was not making any progress, skipped to the next problem. Fortunately, this was a test in which one had to answer only three out of five questions. Several months later, I was working on another paper and in the course of my calculations found myself confronted with a similar problem. This time, however, I was "locked on" to the problem and totally involved in it. Much to my surprise, I was able to solve the same problem that had stumped me on the test, literally in seconds. It felt like the simplest thing in the world, and indeed it was, since in the course of my calculations I was routinely solving problems that were much more complex and difficult.

I use the term "locking on" since this is the subjective feeling that one has in the kind of problem-solving that I am describing. When one is locked on to a problem, there is tremendous, almost sensual joy in solving it. It is possible to go without food and sleep, to dismiss all fatigue, until the problem is solved. Beyond this, it appears that one can call forth intellectual resources of which one is usually totally unaware.

Being locked on to a problem also brings a person into a state of consciousness different from his normal state. A much greater portion of the mind seems to be involved in solving the problem than in a normal mental state. It could therefore be considered a "problem-solving" state of consciousness.

I also remember a period during which I was painting. I had just learned how to use acrylics and had found that I could produce a fairly decent piece of work. Whenever I got involved in a painting, it seemed that I was also "locked on" to the project; I would find it extremely difficult to leave it. Again, I was able to create paintings that were surprising even to me. It appeared that when I was creating, I was going into a higher state of consciousness. Subjectively, I did not simply feel a sense of greater awareness or alertness; rather, I felt as if I were thinking in an entirely different mode.

The difference between ordinary intelligence and genius may not be so much a matter of a person's innate ability as his ability to "lock on" to the work at hand and get into a higher state of consciousness. Ordinary people consider works of genius beyond their reach, but this might not be true, since the creator himself may be surprised at what he produces when in a "locked-on" state of consciousness. The degree of creativity that one has, whether in art or in problem-solving, may be several orders of magnitude greater when one is in a "locked-on" state than when one is in a normal state of consciousness. It may be that the secret of genius is the ability to lock on to problems or creative efforts on a much deeper level than most people ordinarily attain.

This locked-on state of consciousness appears to be associated with increased physical energy. The pulse is quicker, and one may perspire profusely. Sometimes, one even has the experience of trembling with creativity. It seems that while one is in such a state, the energy that one is utilizing is much greater than normal, and not only is the mind completely involved in the creative effort, but also the body.

There appears to be, however, another type of problem-solving consciousness. The first time I became aware of it was when, in the course of Kabbalistic research, I was trying to figure out the properties of a five-dimensional hypercube. The problem was extremely difficult, since it involved trying to visualize what would happen when the hypercube was rotated through five-dimensional space. I had spent several afternoons sweating over the problem, without even coming close to a solution.

Then, one evening, I was relaxing in the bathtub, and my mind wandered to the problem, almost offhandedly. Suddenly, every aspect of the problem seemed perfectly clear, and relationships that had been impossibly complex were now easy to visualize and understand. By the time I got out of the tub, I had worked out the problem completely.

Eventually, I began to realize that this was happening to me often. Sitting in the tub was an excellent time to solve the most difficult problems. But the experience was very different from being locked on to a problem. Quite to the contrary, the mind was free to wander wherever it wanted, but it seemed to hit upon the right answers with surprising clarity.

It seems that the mind has two modes in which it possesses abnormal ability to solve problems. One is the "locked-on" mode, in which the energy of both mind and body is increased. The other is when a person is completely relaxed and the mind drifts to the problem on its own.

I think of the "locked-on" mode as a "hot" mode of thought and the relaxed mode as a "cool" mode of thought. In both cases, one's problem-solving ability is tremendously expanded. In hot concentration, the entire body is brought into play and, as it were, the adrenaline is made to flow. In cool concentration, body and mind are quieted down as much as possible, so that the mind is able to focus on the problem like a laser beam.

These two examples may seem far removed from the usual discussion of the higher states of consciousness associated with meditation. However, there are important links.

First, there are intellectual modes of meditation. In some traditions, they are associated with "the way of the intellect." Some types of meditation appear to be designed to produce precisely the states of consciousness in which problem-solving ability is enhanced.

There is also a direct relationship to the better-known forms of meditation. Mantra meditation, which consists of repeating a word or phrase over and over, is said to elicit the "relaxation response." Many clinical psychologists use this type of meditation to induce relaxation in their patients. Indeed, a type of mantra meditation known as Standardized Clinical Meditation (SCM) has been devised as a therapeutic tool, devoid of all mystical elements.

While this technique appears to relax the body, it also increases the mind's activity. Mantra meditation can be used to relax the body and bring the mind into a state of "cool concentration." When a person is in such a state, his control of his mind processes seems to be increased. This can be demonstrated by a simple experiment:

Sit down in a straight-backed chair. Your back should be straight, since if you are in a hunched or slouched position, you will begin to feel cramped after a while. This experiment should be done at a time when you know that you will not be disturbed or interrupted.

Begin by relaxing completely. Then close your eyes. Initially, you will see lights and images flashing in the mind's eye. After a minute or two, these flashes will begin to coalesce and take the form of kaleidoscopically changing images, as discussed earlier. As you relax, the images will begin to change more and more slowly, and eventually they will remain in the mind's eye long enough for you to focus on them.

Just concentrate on the images. If other thoughts enter the mind, gently push them out. Try to maintain your concentration on the forms that arise in your mind's eye, and on nothing else. Gradually, you should find that you can hold on to an image for quite a while.

The first few times you do this, try to relax and concentrate on the images in your mind's eye without doing anything else. Each session should last for twenty to thirty minutes. Gradually, your ability to hold images and focus on them should increase.

Once you have reached this stage, you are ready to demonstrate to yourself the effects of mantra meditation. Since you are only experimenting, and not making a long-term discipline of it at this point, it does not matter what you use for a mantra. It can consist of a nonsense phrase, a favorite line of poetry, a phrase from the Bible, or any other group of words. Some people find the words "My name is ——" an easy phrase to begin with. If you wish to make a more spiritual experience of it, you can use Rabbi Nachman's mantra, "Lord of the Universe," or its Hebrew equivalent (see chapter 5).

Sitting comfortably, just repeat your experimental mantra over and over. At this point, it does not matter how you repeat it. You may wish to chant it slowly, whisper it, or silently mouth the words. The phrase should be said slowly, over and over again, for the entire session. After a while, you will begin to feel very relaxed and at the same time very alert.

Now, while repeating the mantra, pay attention to the images formed in your mind's eye. As the mind quiets down, these images should become more and more vivid, and you should be able to hold them in the mind for longer and longer periods. The images may become spectacular and beautiful, sometimes even breathtaking.

The images formed in the mind's eye constitute one of the few objective indicators of the meditative state. You know that you are in a meditative state when the imagery in the mind's eye begins to take on a more substantial and permanent form. While imaging is not the only manifestation of higher states of consciousness, it is an indicator that is important and easy to describe objectively. Other indicators are also manifestations of one's control over the mental process, just as visualization is.

Since this is being done as an experiment, it is not advisable to go too far in this direction without carefully planning out a course of meditation. But the experiment shows that in higher states of consciousness, one's ability to form images in the mind and concentrate on them is greatly enhanced.

After progressing in meditation and learning how to concentrate, a process that can take weeks or months, one can learn how
to control the images seen in one's mind's eye. At this point, one
can conjure up an image and hold it in the field of vision as long
as one desires. As we shall see, this in itself can become a form of
meditation.

Earlier, we discussed the random images that appear in the
mind's eye and spoke of them as being a sort of static produced
by the brain. Although this static is most easily seen with the
eyes closed, it also exists when we are looking at things; at that
time, it tends to dull our perception. Thus, if one is looking at a
rose, the experience of the rose's beauty is diminished by this
static.

When a person learns how to hold an image in the mind,
however, he can also control the mind's static. He can then see
things without being disturbed by the brain's self-generated images. This is especially significant in the appreciation of beauty. If
a person "turns off" the mind's static and then looks at a rose, the
image in his mind's eye will contain nothing other than the rose.
Since at this point he can see the rose without any static, the
beauty of the rose is enhanced manyfold. This is one reason that
many people report an enhanced sense of beauty while in the
meditative state. Indeed, many people learn meditation primarily to experience the new aesthetic experiences that can be encountered in such states of consciousness.

Once a person learns how to control the visions in the mind's
eye, he can progress to increasingly more advanced visualizations. The simplest stages of visualization are straightforward;
one conjures up images of figures, letters, objects, or scenes.
What one sees is not much different from what one sees with
normal vision. Nevertheless, to make the images in the mind's
eye appear as solid and real as waking images requires considerable training. As one becomes more advanced, the images can
appear even more real than what one sees with open eyes.

The more advanced one becomes in controlling one's mind,
the more control one has over what one can see in the mind's
eye. When a person becomes expert in visualization, he will be

able to see things in the mind's eye that he could never see with his physical eyes. From descriptions in Kabbalistic and other mystical works, it appears that many experiences encountered in higher states of consciousness fall into this category.

Thus, for example, the Zohar speaks of the "lamp of darkness." This appears to denote a darkness that radiates. Similarly, in Talmudic sources, there are references to "black fire." There is a teaching that the primeval Torah was originally written "with black fire on white fire." This is something that we cannot see with ordinary vision, and indeed, it is impossible to imagine in a normal state of consciousness. Ordinarily, we see bright colors, not blackness or darkness, as radiant.

In the mind's eye, however, it is possible to visualize a lamp radiating darkness. It would be like the negative image of a lamp radiating light. Just as when one sees light, one is aware that energy is being radiated, when one sees the lamp of darkness, one would be aware of negative energy radiating. Visualizing "black fire" would be a very similar experience. When a person has learned to control his visualization experience, negative energy becomes a simple thing to visualize.

It is also possible for a person to intensify his perception of beauty in an image in his mind's eye. This is beyond the enhanced perception that we have discussed earlier, in which one removes the static and focuses the entire mind on a beautiful object. Rather, one would be turning up the "beauty" dial in the mind, to make the mind particularly sensitive and appreciative of beauty. The image that one then sees in the mind's eye may appear thousands of times more beautiful than an image seen with the physical eyes, since one is intentionally amplifying the sensation of beauty.

This is significant, since Beauty (*tifereth*) is one of the Ten Sefiroth discussed in Kabbalah. The Ten Sefiroth are Will (*keter*), Learning Ability (*chokhmah*), Understanding (*binah*), Love (*chesed*), Strength (*gevurah*), Beauty (*tifereth*), Dominance (*netzach*), Submissiveness (*hod*), Sexuality (*yesod*), and Receptivity (*malkhuth*). These Sefiroth may be looked upon as "dials" in the mind that can be used to amplify the experiences associated with them. Thus, since Beauty is one of the Ten Sefiroth, one can turn up the "dial" and amplify the sensation.

Another important phenomenon that can be experienced in a higher, controlled state of consciousness is panoscopic vision. Normally, when one looks at a solid object, one can see only one side of it at a time. Similarly, in the mind's eye, one usually visualizes something only one side at a time. Of course, in the case of a real object, one can rotate it to see the other side, and one can do the same in the mind's eye. In a higher state of consciousness, however, it is possible to attain panoscopic vision, whereby one can look at an object in the mind's eye from all sides at once.

Thus, for example, if one were looking at America on a globe, one would not be able to see Asia, since it is on the opposite side of the globe. However, in a higher state of consciousness, it would be possible to visualize the globe and see America and Asia simultaneously. It is impossible to describe this sensation to one who has never experienced it. A number of modern artists, such as Picasso, seem to have had such experiences and attempted to depict them on canvas.

The human mind can normally visualize an object only from one side because this is the way we see with our eyes. This is merely due to habit from the time of infanthood. When one learns how to control one's mental processes, one can break these habits and visualize things in totally different perspectives. Panoscopic vision is one example of this phenomenon.

There is evidence that the prophet Ezekiel had such an experience in his famous vision. He describes certain angels, known as *chayyoth*, as having four different faces on four different sides: the face of a man, the face of a lion, the face of an ox, and the face of an eagle. Yet he continually stresses that these figures "did not rotate as they moved." What he was saying was that although he saw the *chayyoth* from only one side and they did not rotate, he could see all four faces at once.

Even more spectacular is the fact that in an advanced state of consciousness, it is possible to visualize more than the usual three dimensions. Of course, with our physical eyes, we never see more than the three-dimensional world around us. However, in higher meditative states, it is possible to visualize four and sometimes even five dimensions. There is evidence that the *Sefer Yetzirah* (Book of Creation) contains meditative exercises that include such visualizations.

Synesthesia is another important phenomenon observed in higher states of consciousness. Human senses tend to be compartmentalized, so that different parts of the mind deal with different senses; one part of the mind may deal with sight, while another deals with hearing. In a normal state of consciousness, we do not see sounds or hear colors.

In higher states of consciousness, however, the barriers between the senses are lowered. In such states, one's sense of sight can be used to perceive sounds. Similarly, one is able to hear colors, see fragrances, and feel sights. This is the experience of synesthesia, which means "mixing of senses."

Even in a normal state of consciousness, on an ethereal level, one may have a vague feeling that a sound or melody has a particular texture or color. This is because the barriers between the senses are never totally absolute. In higher states of consciousness, however, the spillover can become quite vivid. For example, one may see a piece of music as a complex visual pattern. I am saying not that the music is *associated* with the pattern, but that the music *is* the pattern. It is a very strange sensation, which is impossible to describe to someone who has never experienced it.

There is Talmudic evidence that synesthesia was associated with the mystical state of revelation. When the Ten Commandments were given, the Torah describes the people's experience by stating, "All the people *saw* the sounds" (Exod. 20:18). An ancient Talmudic source states that "they saw that which would normally be heard, and heard that which would normally be seen." This is a clear example of synesthesia.

Another phenomenon that can be visualized in a higher meditative state is nothingness. When we think of nothingness, we often think of it as simple blackness, a vacuum, or the interplanetary void. None of this, however, is true nothingness. Blackness or space cannot be nothingness, since "blackness" and "space" are things themselves. Nothingness must be the absence of everything, even of blackness and empty space.

If you want to know what nothingness looks like, just focus on what you see behind your head. (In some systems, one focuses on what one sees *inside* the head.) Obviously, you cannot see anything behind your head. But this means precisely that what you see behind your head is nothingness. Therefore, if you want to know what nothing really looks like, concentrate on what you see behind your head.

If you wanted to visualize nothingness in a meditative state, you would have to take this perception of nothingness and bring it into your mind's eye. In a normal state of consciousness, this would be impossible, but in higher states of consciousness, with training and practice, it can be accomplished. Indeed, in a number of systems of meditation, it is an important practice.

For one thing, filling the mind with nothingness is a highly effective way of clearing it of all perception. There are some experiences that are so subtle that even the visualization of blackness or empty space could overshadow them. However, when the mind is filled with the experience of nothingness, it is open to the most subtle influences.

One of the influences that the mind can detect while visualizing nothingness is the spiritual. In such a state, the spiritual can appear very spectacular, since the nothingness in the mind can be filled with that which comes from the Without.

Of course, visualizing nothingness is a highly advanced technique. The spiritual, however, can be experienced on much simpler levels. Indeed, there appears to be an area of the mind that is particularly receptive to the spiritual experience. Sometimes, without warning, a person can have a spiritual experience that leaves him awestruck or exhilarated. A more intense spiritual experience can have a profound effect on a person's entire life.

Just as a person can amplify his sense of beauty through meditation, he can also amplify his sense of the spiritual. If part of the mind is particularly sensitive to the spiritual, then through meditation this sensitivity can voluntarily be enhanced and increased.

This results from the control of the mind that one has during the meditative experience.

Enhanced spiritual experiences are associated with the states of consciousness experienced by prophets and mystics. The senses are blocked out, and all sensation, both internal and external, is eliminated. In such states of consciousness, the feeling of the Divine is strengthened, and a person can experience an intense feeling of closeness to God. Meditations of this type can bring a person to the most profound and beautiful experiences imaginable.

A word of caution is in order at this point. The experiences that a person can have in these states of consciousness can be so beatific that he may not want to return to his normal state of consciousness. It is possible for a person to become completely lost in the mystic state, acutally swallowed up by it. Therefore, before exploring these highest states, be sure that you have something to bring you down safely. It is very much like flying a plane. Taking off is exhilarating, but before you take off, you had better know how to land again.

For this reason, most texts on Jewish meditation stress that before embarking on the higher levels, a person should have a master. Then, if he goes "up" and does not know how to come down, or does not want to, the master will be able to talk him down.

Other sources indicate that mystics would actually take an oath to return to a normal state of consciousness at the end of their meditative sessions. Then, even if they were not inclined to return, they would be bound by their oath.

All texts on Jewish meditation stress that the person embarking on more advanced forms of meditation should first develop a strong internal discipline. This is very important, since higher states of consciousness are very enticing and it is possible to lose one's sense of reality. However, if a person is in control of his actions and emotions in general, he will also remain in control of his sense of reality. Rather than negate his life, his meditative experiences will enhance it.

It is in this context that a common folk saying states that people who study Kabbalah go mad. This obviously does not mean the academic study of Kabbalah; although Kabbalah is a difficult intellectual discipline, it is no more dangerous than any other study. However, involvement in the more esoteric forms of Kabbalistic meditation can be dangerous to mental health, especially if the meditator proceeds without adequate preparation.

In a sense, it is like climbing a mountain. Even for an experienced climber, there is always an element of danger. If a person had limited experience, he would not even think of climbing a difficult mountain without a guide; to do so would be to court disaster. The same is true of one who tries the more esoteric forms of meditation without proper training and discipline.

The forms of meditation presented in this book are not dangerous mountains. Rather, they are gentle hills, which are safe to climb, but from which one can see wide vistas.

5. Jewish Meditation

In the previous chapters, we have discussed the discipline of meditation in general. Before we can understand Jewish meditation, we must first have a good idea of the nature of meditation in its broadest sense. The phenomenology and psychology of Jewish meditation are not particularly different from those of other systems. The goals and results, however, are often very different.

There is ample evidence that meditative practices were widespread among Jews throughout Jewish history. References to meditation are found in major Jewish texts in every period from the biblical to the premodern era. One reason that this has not been universally recognized is that the vocabulary of meditation has been lost to a large degree, especially during the last century.

Until the rise of the Jewish Enlightenment, mysticism and intellectualism had equal status within Judaism. The ostensible goal of the Enlightenment, however, was to raise the intellectual level of Judaism, and positive as this may have been, it was often done at the expense of other Jewish values. The first values to fall by the wayside were Jewish mysticism in general and meditation in particular. Anything that touched upon the mystical was denigrated as superstition and occultism and was deemed unworthy of serious study.

Even Kabbalah, which contains mysticism par excellence, was reduced to simply an intellectual exercise; its deeper meanings were totally lost. In earlier chapters we discussed how many phenomena experienced in a meditative state cannot be understood rationally. This premise was not recognized by the nineteenth-century rationalists, and even the ineffable became the subject of philosophical discussion.

For this and other reasons, all references to meditation vanished from mainstream Jewish literature about 150 years ago. This is true even in Chasidic literature, where meditation initially played a central role. Because of this antimystical trend, even Kabbalistic works published after around 1840 show a surprising lack of even the slightest mention of meditation. After a century of indifference, even the meanings of key words were forgotten.

In earlier literature, by contrast, references to meditation are abundant. This is true even in the Bible, although one has to resort to a kind of "verbal archaeology" to discover the true meaning of key words.

In any case, it appears from both biblical and postbiblical sources that meditation was central to the prophetic experience, and that this experience was attained in the meditative state. The Bible states explicitly that the prophets used chants and music to attain higher states of consciousness. Careful philological analysis of certain key words in the Bible suggests that they refer to specific meditative methods. This subject formed the basis of my first book on the subject, *Meditation and the Bible*. However, since the discussion consists largely of analysis of Hebrew words, it is beyond the scope of this book.

From the literature, it seems evident that a prophet would almost always experience his first prophetic experience while in a meditative state. Later, however, it would become possible for him to experience prophecy without meditation. Sometimes prophecy would come to a prophet unexpectedly and without warning. This probably involved a phenomenon sometimes referred to as "flashback." After a person has become adept at reaching higher levels of consciousness through meditation, he can occasionally reach such levels spontaneously as well. This seems to be evident in the experiences of a number of prophets.

There is also evidence that during the period when the Bible was written (until approximately 400 B.C.E.), meditation was practiced by a large proportion of the Israelite people. The Talmud and Midrash state explicitly that over a million people were involved in such disciplines. Regular schools of meditation existed, led by master prophets. The master prophets, in turn, were under the leadership of the primary prophets, the ones actually quoted in the Bible. In these schools, people were taught meditative methods in order to attain a closeness to God; as a side effect of such meditation, prophecy was also sometimes achieved.

Since nonprophets may have been practicing meditators, they would also experience spontaneous prophecy or visions, without actually meditating. This would explain the biblical accounts of individuals who had prophetic visions even though they were not meditating and had no prior prophetic experience. When a person engages in meditation on a regular basis, he can reach meditative states of consciousness spontaneously, without meditation, and these states can cause him to experience visions.

Everything found in later literature seems to indicate that these meditative schools required a strong discipline and faithful adherence to a strict regimen. The schools were extremely demanding, and were open only to those willing to devote themselves totally. Before even being admitted to one of these ancient meditative schools, a person had to be not only spiritually advanced but in complete control of all his emotions and feelings. Beyond that, the disciplines of the Torah and commandments were central to these schools, and these disciplines required a degree of self-mastery to which not everyone could aspire.

It appears that this was one of the attractions of ancient idolatry. While the Jewish meditative schools required extensive discipline and preparation, many idolatrous schools of mysticism and meditation were open to all. A person could at least think that he was having a transcendental experience, without adhering to the tight discipline of Torah and Judaism. It was very much like the situation today, when Eastern meditative groups seem easier to relate to than the strict discipline of Judaism.

For anyone who has ever had a taste of the transcendental, it can be an infinitely sweet experience, more pleasurable than love or sex. For many people, it was an experience after which they would actually lust. When the Talmud speaks of the "lust for idolatry," it could be speaking of the magnetic attraction that this spiritual experience had for people. If they could not get it from Israelite sources, they would seek it in idolatrous rites.

As long as the Israelites were in their homeland, the situation was more or less under control. Idolatry may have been a strong temptation, but the prophetic mystical schools were strong enough to unite the people and prevent them from assimilating. Even if individuals or groups backslid, they could always be drawn back into the fold. In sum, during the entire First Commonwealth, meditation and mysticism played a central role in Judaism; the spiritual leaders were the prophets, the individuals who were most advanced spiritually.

All this changed with the diaspora, which scattered Jews all over the world. It was realized that if the masses remained involved in prophetic mysticism, the temptations drawing them to idolatry would ultimately alienate them from the Torah. Isolated, widely scattered groups would be ready prey to false teachers and experiences. Therefore, around this time, the more advanced forms of meditation were hidden from the masses and made part of a secret teaching. Now only the most qualified individuals would be party to the secrets of advanced prophetic meditation.

One of the last of the great prophets was Ezekiel, who lived in Babylonia right at the beginning of the Exile. The first chapter of the Book of Ezekiel is one of the most mysterious parts of the entire Bible. In it, the prophet describes his visions of angels and the Divine Throne in extraordinary detail. According to one tradition, this vision contained the keys to prophetic meditation and, if understood, could serve as a guide to attaining prophecy. The study of this chapter became known as the "discipline of the chariot" (*maaseh merkavah*). The methodology was there, but without the key it could not be understood.

By the time of the rebuilding of the Second Temple, and the

establishment of the Second Commonwealth, the Jewish leadership was clearly aware of the dangers that chariot meditation posed if it were made available to the masses. First, without adequate teachers and masters, Jews living in the diaspora would pervert the methods or use them for the wrong ends. This in turn could lead to the splintering of Judaism into rival sects or to the establishment of religions alien to Judaism. The net result would be the disunification of the Jewish people.

Second, as discussed earlier, Jewish meditation was an extremely difficult discipline, which required years of preparation. If it were an accepted part of Judaism, it was feared that Jews would become frustrated by the difficulties of practicing it and be tempted to try non-Jewish forms of meditation. This, in turn, could lead them to idolatry and assimilation. Idolatry had been enough of a problem during the First Commonwealth, when all the Israelites were in their homeland; now, in the diaspora, there was a distinct danger that it would lead to the destruction of the entire nation.

Therefore, the Jewish leadership made a very difficult decision. The benefits of having the masses involved in the highest types of meditation were weighed against the dangers. Although the nation might lose a degree of spirituality as a result of the decision, it would at least survive. Henceforth, the discipline of the chariot had to be made into a secret doctrine, taught only to the most select individuals. The Great Assembly, which represented the first Jewish leadership in the Second Commonwealth, thus decreed: "The discipline of the chariot may be taught only to individual students (one at a time), and they must be wise, understanding with their own knowledge."

The Great Assembly also realized that the general populace would need a meditative discipline. But rather than have it be something loose and unstructured, they needed a discipline with a structure common to the entire Jewish nation, one that would serve as a means of uniting the people. It would have to contain the hopes and aspirations of the nation as a whole, to reinforce the unity of the Jewish people.

The meditative discipline that was composed by the Great

Assembly ended up as the Amidah, a "standing" prayer consisting of eighteen sections, which would be repeated silently, in an upright position, three times each day. It is true that nowadays the Amidah is thought of more as a prayer than a meditative device, but the most ancient sources regard it as a meditation. Indeed, the Talmud verifies that this was its original intention.

This also explains why the Great Assembly legislated that the same prayer be repeated three times each day. People often complain that saying the same prayer over and over is tedious and uninspiring. For anyone familiar with mantra meditation, however, the opposite is true. All types of mantra meditation involve repetition. In mantra meditation, the device repeated is a word or a phrase, and it can be repeated over and over for weeks, months, or even years on end.

The Amidah was meant to be repeated three times every day from childhood on, and essentially the same formula would be said for an entire lifetime. The Amidah could therefore be looked upon as one long mantra. In many ways, it has the same effects as a mantra, lifting the individual to a high meditative level of consciousness. As we shall, there is an entire literature that describes how the Amidah can be used in this manner. But most important, there is ample evidence that it was originally composed as the common form of meditation to be used by the entire Jewish nation.

From Talmudic times through the Middle Ages, an extensive literature dealing with Jewish meditation was written. Virtually every method found in general meditation can be found in ancient Jewish texts, as well as a number of methods that are found nowhere else. Indeed, a comparative study of meditative methods shows that the Jewish systems may have been among the most advanced in the world.

The Talmud speaks at length of meditation and meditative experiences, referring to it as the discipline of the chariot or "entering Paradise." There are numerous anecdotes about Talmudic sages, such as Rabban Yochanan ben Zakkai and Rabbi Akiva, engaging in these practices. The Talmud also says that the "original saints" (*chasidim rishonim*) spent an hour reciting the

Amidah; the context shows that it is speaking of a meditative rather than a worship experience. However, since meditation had become a secret doctrine within Judaism by Talmudic times, everything is couched in allusion and allegory. Only to one who is aware of the methods do the accounts even begin to make sense.

There were two major works on meditation that were most probably published during the Talmudic period (around 100–500 C.E.). The first is the *Sefer Yetzirah*, the Book of Creation. This is the most enigmatic text on Jewish mysticism. Over a hundred commentaries have been written on this text in an effort to un-ravel its mysteries, but they all tend to read their own systems into the text rather than extract its message. Careful analysis of the text, however, shows it to be an extremely advanced work on meditation.

Another important text from this period is *Heykhaloth Rabba-tai* (Greater Book of the [Divine] Chambers). This is a primary text on *merkavah* mysticism, which describes some of the tech-niques used in the discipline of the chariot. This work is fairly explicit, but even here, unless one is familiar with meditative techniques, the text is largely opaque.

In the Middle Ages, meditation was a well-known technique and was discussed at length by the Jewish philosophers, espe-cially in connection with prophecy. Such Jewish philosophers as Maimonides and Gersonides analyzed the meditative state in depth, contrasting the visions that one has in a meditative state with those in a dream state. The way it is discussed suggests that meditation was considered an integral part of Judaism.

Among Jewish mystics and Kabbalists, it was evident that meditation played a key role. A great deal was written during this period about experiences that one could have in the meditative state and how one's vision and state of conscious could be altered. Techniques were alluded to, but always in veiled hints, as if this teaching was bound to remain an oral tradition, never be put in writing. With one exception, we are left with tantalizing allu-sions, but no clear facts.

The one individual who broke the rule of secrecy was Abraham

Abulafia (1240–1296). He was a highly controversial figure for many reasons, not the least being the fact that he felt he was destined to be either a messianic figure or a harbinger of the Messiah. But, as he states explicitly in his works, he was the first to put the methods of Kabbalah meditation into writing. Although he was criticized in his time, later Kabbalists recognized that the methods he describes represent the true tradition of prophetic Kabbalism.

Soon after Abulafia's time an event was to occur that would eclipse meditation as the focus of Kabbalah. This was the publication of the Zohar in the 1290s. Although this mystical work contains many allusions to meditative methods, it does not speak explicitly about meditation. But the spiritual systems described by the Zohar are so complex that it would take a lifetime to understand them—and this is exactly what happened.

With the publication of the Zohar, Kabbalah entered a new era. Besides reaching mystical states and higher states of consciousness, Kabbalists now had a new goal, namely to understand the Zohar. This made Kabbalah into an academic discipline as well as a mystical one. One begins to find more and more books published on Kabbalah that regard it as a philosophy rather than as an experience. Indeed, by the fifteenth century, it was virtually impossible to write a book on Jewish philosophy without referring to the Kabbalah.

The mystical element, however, was still very important. Kabbalah study reached its zenith in the famed community of Safed, the city of saints and mystics. Foremost among the Safed Kabbalists was Rabbi Isaac Luria (1534–1572), usually referred to as the Ari. He was so spiritually sensitive that he became a legend in his own lifetime, but his main accomplishment was the vast body of Kabbalistic literature that he bequeathed to the world. The Ari unraveled the mystery of the Zohar, showing how its system could form the basis of a meditative discipline. Beyond that, he left a system of Kabbalah that is one of the most complex intellectual systems devised by man.

This, in turn, had the effect of further intellectualizing Kabbalah, making the mystical realm every bit as stimulating and fascinating as philosophy or Talmud. Thus, Kabbalah gained status as an intellectual discipline in its own right. The works of Kabbalists in the seventeenth and eighteenth centuries took their place as some of the most profound, complex, and challenging Judaic works ever written. But this phenomenon also had the effect of reducing the importance of meditation, even among Jewish mystics. For many, Jewish mysticism and Kabbalah had become an intellectual exercise and nothing more.

There was yet another influence that downgraded the importance of Kabbalah in this period. This was the reaction to the false messiah, Sabbatai Zvi (1626–1676). This charismatic individual twisted the teachings of Kabbalah and used it to support his warped messianic claims. His career ended when he was challenged by the Turkish sultan; he chose to convert to Islam rather than suffer martyrdom, leaving thousands of his followers totally disillusioned. The false messiah gave mysticism a bad name and brought about the eclipse of Jewish mysticism and meditation for almost a century.

A renaissance of Jewish mysticism occurred in the middle of the eighteenth century under the leadership of the famed Rabbi Israel, known as the Baal Shem Tov (1698–1760). The Chasidic movement, which he founded, was based on mysticism, and meditative exercises were central to the movement. An important early Chasidic technique involved using the daily service as a meditative exercise. Not only did the Chasidic movement bring meditation back into Judaism, but it infused the Jewish community with new energy and commitment as well.

Still, the established Jewish community saw the embryonic Chasidic movement as a threat. Since it had adopted unique and distinctive practices, many Jewish leaders felt that the movement could become a cult. It was also felt that the movement was too closely associated with a single personality, a trait reminiscent of the Sabbatai Zvi fiasco. A powerful opposition to Chasidism arose, going so far as to excommunicate the entire movement. Leading rabbinical sages throughout Europe were marshaled to express their opposition to the movement in the strongest terms.

This, in turn, had its effect on the Chasidic movement. Some elements of this movement took a road that had been traveled earlier, reducing all its mystical teachings to philosophy. Others chose to institutionalize the role of spiritual master, making allegiance to a master (or *rebbe*) the main distinguishing feature of Chasidism.

During the first three generations of Chasidism, there was hardly a published work on the subject that did not contain some mention of meditation and the mystical experience. In later works, however, mysticism is notably lacking. Indeed, in many areas, after 1850, the Chasidic movement developed a strong antimystical trend. Thus, one of the last bastions of Jewish meditation fell, and the entire practice was forgotten for over a century. Even the basic vocabulary of meditation seemed to have been lost. Scholars wrote about Jewish mysticism but ignored blatant references to meditation; key words for meditation were either mistranslated or misinterpreted. A situation arose in which meditation was virtually erased from the Jewish consciousness and obliterated from Jewish history.

At this point it would be useful to discuss the most common terms for meditation found in Jewish texts. Since all of these texts were written in Hebrew, the key words are also in that language. From their roots and form, considerable insight can be obtained into the types of meditation that they signify.

The most common word for meditation in Judaic literature is *kavanah*. This word is translated as "concentration" or "feeling" or "devotion." In context, the literature speaks of worshiping with *kavanah* or maintaining *kavanah* while performing a sacred act. However, looking at the origin of the word *kavanah*, we immediately see that it comes from the Hebrew root *kaven*, which means "to aim." Therefore, *kavanah* denotes "aiming" consciousness toward a certain goal. The most apt translation is "directed consciousness."

Earlier, we defined meditation as controlled thinking. In this sense, *kavanah* would be the most generic Hebrew term for meditation.

The word *kavanah* is most often used in relation to prayer or worship. In Judaism, as we shall see, the line between worship and meditation is often a very fine one. Many elements of the worship service are specifically designed to be used as meditations, to reacher higher states of consciousness. We have discussed this usage with regard to the Amidah, but it is also true of a number of other prayers.

When one has *kavanah* in worship, one is allowing the words of the service to direct one's consciousness. The mind is brought to the state of consciousness defined by the prayer one is reciting. In this respect, the prayer is used to direct the consciousness.

The word *kavanah* is also associated with various actions, especially those involving fulfillment of the commandments or rituals. Here, too, *kavanah* denotes clearing the mind of extraneous thought and concentrating totally on the action at hand. The act itself becomes the means through which the person's consciousness is directed.

In addition to the general concept of *kavanah*, various Jewish devotional works, especially those of a Kabbalistic nature, contain collections of specific *kavanah* meditations, or *kavanoth*, for various rituals. These *kavanoth* are used to direct the mind along the inner paths defined by the esoteric meaning of the ritual.

Another important Hebrew term associated with meditation is *hitbonenuth*. Translated literally, this word means "self-understanding." It reflects a somewhat different type of meditation.

Normally, we look at things dispassionately and objectively. I may look at a leaf and even examine it very closely, but it does not affect me in any way. I am exactly the same person after as I was before. It does not change my state of consciousness at all. My mind is the same looking at the leaf as it would be otherwise.

However, I may also look at the leaf with the aim of using it to attain a higher level of consciousness or a greater degree of self-awareness. I would then be using the leaf as a means to achieve "self-understanding," or *hitbonenuth*.

The great Jewish philosopher Moses Maimonides (1135–1204) speaks about using *hitbonenuth* meditation while contemplating God's creation. One can achieve a profound love for God through such contemplation. This is effective precisely because it is not

merely a simple contemplation of various aspects of God's creation, but is understanding oneself as part of this creation. When
one sees God's creation, and understands one's own role as part
of it, one can develop a deep and lasting love for God. Who has
not gone out into the fields on a clear night and gazed at the stars,
yearning to unlock their secret? One thinks about the vast, un-
fathomable reaches of the universe and stands in rapt awe. For
many people, this in itself can be a "religious experience." It is an
experience that can bring a person to feel a profound humility
before the infinite vastness of the universe.

The next step is to go beyond the physical and contemplate the
fact that this vast universe, with all its countless stars and galaxies, was all created by God. One ponders the fact that one ineffable Being created everything. We realize how different this
Being must be from us, and yet we feel a certain closeness.

The final step is *hitbonenuth*, understanding oneself in the
light of this vast creation. At this level, one asks the questions, "If
God created this vast universe, then who am I? How do I fit into
all of this?" At the same time, one may feel privileged that God
allows us to have a direct relationship with Him. Imagine that the
creator of all the stars and galaxies deigns to listen to me! Not
only that, but He is concerned about me! Realizing God's greatness, and at the same time contemplating the closeness to Him
that He allows us to enjoy, is precisely what can bring a person to
profound love for God.

The Psalmist expressed this when he said, "I look at Your
heavens, the work of Your fingers, the moon and stars that You
have established. What is man that You remember him, a son of
Adam that You even consider him? Yet, You have made him a
little less than divine, You have adorned him with glory and
honor. You made him master over all Your creatures and placed
everything under his feet" (Ps. 8:4–6). We realize how insignifi-
cant we should be in God's eyes, and yet how significant we
really are.

Hitbonenuth meditation can be focused on anything—a stone,
a leaf, a flower, or an idea. One allows the subject to fill the mind
and then uses it as a means to understand the self. It is a type of

mirror in which one can see oneself in the light of true Reality. Using this mirror, one can see the Divine within oneself. Indeed, this may be the "mirror [*aspaklaria*] of prophecy" described in the Talmud. When one looks into this mirror and sees the Divine within oneself, one can also communicate with the Divine.

The final important Hebrew word for meditation is *hitbodeduth*. This is the most specific term for meditation and one that was used as early as the tenth century. Literally, the word means "self-isolation," and for this reason, the term escaped the notice of many students of Jewish mysticism. Many scholars have translated *hitbodeduth* simply as "seclusion" or "isolation," not realizing that it refers to meditation.

The key to this term is to be found in a text by Moses Maimonides' son, Abraham. He writes that there are two types of isolation, external self-isolation and internal self-isolation. External self-isolation simply involves being alone physically—going off to fields, woods, or caves, anywhere away from other people. This, however, is only the first step; external self-isolation is the doorway to internal self-isolation.

Internal self-isolation consists in isolating the mind from all outward sensation and then even from thought itself. From what one reads in most non-Jewish classical texts, this is what is usually defined as the meditative state. Therefore, *hitbodeduth* is the Hebrew term for any practice that brings a person into the meditative state. It is a state in which the mind is isolated, standing alone, without any sensation or thought.

It is known that sensory deprivation can help a person attain higher states of consciousness. Indeed, there are places in large cities where a person can buy time in a sensory deprivation chamber. In such a perfectly dark, soundproof chamber, one floats in a dense liquid at body temperature. Cut off completely from all outward stimuli, the mind can go off totally on its own and float toward higher states of consciousness.

True meditation, however, does not require a sensory deprivation chamber. Rather, by using a meditative practice, one can blank out all outside stimuli at will. At the same time, one also blanks out all extraneous thought, filling the mind with the subject of one's meditation. This is *hitbodeduth*, self-isolation in a meditative sense.

Vocabulary is very important, since without it one can read a Hebrew meditative text and not even be aware of the nature of the subject. One reason that people were unaware of the importance and influence of meditation in Judaism is that they were incorrectly translating key words in the most important texts.

The general impression one gains from studying these texts is not only that meditation was practiced by Jews, but that for quite a number of centuries it was a very important ingredient of Judaism. Clearly, Jewish meditation has been part and parcel of Judaism throughout the ages.

6·Mantra Meditation

The best-known form of meditation today is mantra meditation. The word "mantra" is an Eastern term denoting a word or phrase that is repeated over and over as a meditative exercise. In many types of Eastern meditation, mantra meditation is the central exercise, and it forms virtually the entire basis of Transcendental Meditation. Since there is no adequate generic Western term for this type of meditation, I shall use the Eastern term "mantra."

One immediate effect of mantra meditation is to relax the body. In this form of meditation, it seems that the more the body relaxes, the more active the mind becomes. It is as if energy is released by the body, which can be used by the mind.

In any case, meditation, especially using a mantra, is an excellent relaxation method. For this reason, a number of psychologists have developed religiously neutral forms of mantra meditation to elicit the "relaxation response." An entire system called Standardized Clinical Meditation (SCM) has been developed to utilize this form of meditation in a clinical context.

Mantra meditation most probably works largely through habituation. If a person is in a room all day with, say, a loudly ticking clock, his mind eventually turns off the sound of the ticking. Although he hears the ticking, it simply does not register. The person is said to have become habituated to the ticking sound, so that he no longer pays attention to it. This is an important mechanism through which the mind filters out the commonplace and allows the thinker to concentrate on what is important.

When one repeats a mantra over and over, the mind also becomes habituated to it. Eventually, one becomes able to say it without the words registering in the conscious mind. By this time, one has also formed the habit of erasing all thought from the mind while reciting the mantra. It is therefore a highly effective psychological means of removing all thought from the mind.

This may seem quite mundane and nonmystical. However, the mantra does not necessarily have to be the mystical element in the meditation. The mantra can serve as a means of clearing the mind of mundane thought, leaving it open to other, transcendental experiences. This can be true no matter how nonmystical the mantra is. Indeed, in certain types of clinical meditation, a nonsense word can be used as the mantra.

Nevertheless, if the mantra has spiritual power in its own right, it not only clears the mind of mundane thought, but also puts the meditator into a special spiritual space. The form of the mantra can be extremely important if one wishes to accomplish a specific spiritual goal in one's meditation.

Although mantra meditation is not the most typical Jewish form of meditation, it is one of the simplest. As in general meditation, it consists in repeating a word or a phrase over and over, usually for a period of half an hour each day. The most important element of the meditation is that it be done daily and that there be a commitment to continue the practice for a period of at least a month. It usually takes between thirty and forty days for the results of this type of meditation to become manifest.

There appear to be references to mantra meditation even in the Bible. On the basis of philological analysis, it seems that the Hebrew verb *hagah* denotes a kind of meditation in which a word or sound is repeated over and over. The great Hebrew linguist David Kimchi (1160–1235) writes that the word *hagah* denotes a sound or a thought that is repeated like the cooing of a dove or the growling of a lion. Nevertheless, the biblical references to this type of meditation are ambiguous and not clearly stated.

The earliest unambiguous reference to a mantra type of meditation is found in *Heykhaloth Rabbatai*, the primary text of Merkavah mysticism, dating from Talmudic times. The text presents
a mystical "name" of God, which is actually a rather long phrase
consisting of a number of mystical words or names. The instruc-
tion says that this phrase must be repeated 120 times, again and
again. The technique is reminiscent of mantra meditation, especially in some Eastern systems in which the mantra is repeated
for a set number of times.

It is significant that in the *Heykhaloth*, the mantra is seen not
as an end in itself, but rather as the first step in the discipline of
the chariot. The mantra was used to bring the initiate into a state
of consciousness from which he could travel from chamber to
chamber in the supernal worlds. Thus, rather than define the
state of consciousness, the mantra brought the individual into the
first stage of the meditative state, from which he could use other
techniques to progress further.

In later Kabbalistic schools, it appears that biblical verses or
selections from the Talmud or Zohar would be used as mantras.
In sixteenth-century Safed, for example, there is mention of a
technique known as *gerushin*, which appears to consist in repeating a biblical verse over and over as a sort of mantra. Besides
bringing the meditator into a higher state of consciousness, the
purpose of this technique was to provide him with deeper insight
into the verse itself. As he repeated the verse, it would eventually appear as if the verse itself were telling the initiate its meaning. Rather than studying or analyzing the verse, the meditator
would then be communing with it.

This concept is even more graphically illustrated in a technique used by Rabbi Joseph Caro (1488–1575) and his followers. Instead of using a biblical verse, this technique made
use of a selection from the Mishnah, the earliest portion of the
Talmud, completed around 200 C.E. A portion of the Mishnah
(a particular paragraph or *mishnah*) would be repeated as a
mantra, leading to a state of consciousness in which a *maggid*,
an angelic being associated with the *mishnah*, would speak to
the meditator. Again, the meditator would gain deep insights,

not from studying or analyzing the *mishnah*, but by experiencing its spiritual essence.

It is significant that there may be an allusion to this technique in the Talmud itself. The Talmud speaks of reviewing a *mishnah* and says, "Repeating one's *mishnah* one hundred times is not the same as repeating it one hundred and one times." There may be an allusion in this teaching that even in Talmudic times, the Mishnah was used as a type of mantra.

There is also evidence that the Ari (Rabbi Isaac Luria) made use of a similar technique with the Zohar. Unlike other Kabbalists of his time, who analyzed the Zohar and tried to probe its mysteries intellectually, the Ari probed its depths by means of a meditative technique. Judging by the description of his technique, he seems to have used a short selection of the Zohar as a mantra, repeating it over and over until its meaning became clear. The Ari describes this experience by saying that the Zohar "spoke to him."

In relatively modern times, a practical form of mantra meditation was prescribed by the noted Chasidic leader Rabbi Nachman of Bratslav (1772–1811). Of all the Chasidic masters, none spoke of *hitbodeduth* meditation more often than he. As we shall see, his main technique consisted in engaging in conversations with God. Nevertheless, Rabbi Nachman said that if a person does not known what to say, he should simply repeat the phrase *Ribbono shel Olam*, which is Hebrew for "Master of the Universe." From the description of the technique, it seems obvious that Rabbi Nachman was prescribing the use of this phrase as a mantra to bring a person into a higher state of consciousness.

Here, too, Rabbi Nachman did not regard repeating the mantra as an end in itself. Rather, he saw it as a way of opening the mind in order to enter into conversation with God, a method that he maintained was the best way to get close to God. Still, he saw repetition as an important technique in its own right.

Since the phrase *Ribbono shel Olam* was prescribed as a mantralike device by Rabbi Nachman, some people refer to it as Rabbi Nachman's mantra. Some, for the sake of authenticity, prefer the Chasidic pronunciation, *Ribboinoi shel Oylawm*. In any case, it is an ideal phrase for anyone who wants to engage in an authentic Jewish mantra meditation. Not only was it prescribed by one of the great Chasidic masters, but the phrase itself was used as an introduction to prayer as far back as early Talmudic times. The expression *Ribbono shel Olam* was used as early as the first century B.C.E. by Simeon ben Shetach, and according to the Talmud, it was also in use in biblical times.

Mantra meditation is one of the simplest types of meditation. It is therefore a good place to begin if you wish to embark on a program of meditation. Rabbi Nachman's mantra, *Ribbono shel Olam,* is a good one with which to start. It also provides an excellent example of meditation in general.

You cannot begin a program of meditation without a certain degree of commitment. In order for it to have an effect, you must do it on a daily basis, spending at least twenty or thirty minutes repeating the mantra. If you do it every day, the effects become cumulative. However, when you miss or skip days, the cumulative effect is lost. Furthermore, it takes several weeks of discipline with a mantra to attain a full level of a higher state of consciousness. Some effects may be manifest immediately, but it takes a few weeks before you experience the full effects. If you have the commitment, the results can be striking.

At this point, a word of warning is in order. Mantra meditation is a fairly safe method for most people, but it can be dangerous for someone with a history of mental illness. If a person's connection to the real world is not strong to begin with, he may have difficulty reestablishing his connection with reality after a deep meditative experience. Just as certain forms of strenuous exercise must be avoided by people with a history of heart trouble, certain forms of mental exercise should be avoided by people with a history of mental illness. The Talmudic story of Ben Zoma, who lost his mind after a particularly intense meditative experience, serves as a warning. Any person with doubts about his mental stability should make sure that he has an expert guide before becoming involved with any type of intense meditation.

In general, the preparations for meditation are straightforward and simple. You should meditate in a time and place where you will not be interrupted or disturbed by people, phone calls, or noise. Rabbi Nachman said that it was best to have a special room for meditation if possible. Since this is a luxury that few can afford, you may choose a special corner of the house, a special chair, or a room where you can be alone at night when no one else is about. Rabbi Nachman also said that woods, hills, and fields are good places to meditate, especially when the weather is comfortable.

But the place is not important, as long as it is an environment where you will not be interrupted. You can even meditate under the covers in bed at night, if it is a place where you know you will not be disturbed, and Rabbi Nachman presents this as a viable alternative. An excellent place, if available, would also be the synagogue when no one is around to disturb the meditative session.

Many people associate meditation with the Eastern lotus position. However, we should remember that in the East it was common to sit on the floor or on a mat, so that the lotus position was close to the normal, comfortable sitting position for Eastern meditators. For Westerners, this position is difficult to learn and is initially quite uncomfortable. In practice, it is found that sitting in a comfortable straight-backed chair is just as effective.

In any case, this is of little relevance to Jewish meditation, since the systems do not prescribe any special position. It is true that there are references to sitting in a chair, but they are only meant as a suggestion. You may choose any position in which you can remain comfortable for a long period of time without moving the body or being subject to cramping.

During meditation, sit with the eyes lightly closed, totally relaxed. Your hands can rest comfortably on the table or on your lap. Your fingers should not be clasped or intertwined, as the Kabbalists teach that this should be avoided. Rather, if your hands are together, one should rest lightly on the other.

Before beginning a meditation, settle yourself in the place. This means sitting quietly in the place where you will be meditating, fitting into it and making yourself at ease. During this period, try to relax completely, clearing your mind of all extraneous concerns. Some people find it helpful to hum a relaxing melody during these preparatory moments. This period should last between five and ten minutes.

In this respect, the advantage of meditating in the same place every day becomes clear. You will come to associate that place with the serene mood developed during meditation, and after a few days, the calmness comes automatically as soon as you sit down in your meditation place. This tends to reinforce the process and make it easier to advance.

Let us assume that you are using Rabbi Nachman's mantra, *Ribbono shel Olam*. Repeat the phrase over and over, slowly, in a very soft voice. The meditative norm is that it should be said in the softest voice that you can comfortably pronounce. You can either whisper it or vocalize it softly, whichever is more comfortable to you.

There are no firm standards regarding this in Jewish meditation. Some people find it easier to whisper the mantra. It is also permissible to mouth it without voicing it at all. It is not recommended, however, that it merely be thought in the mind, at least for beginners. If the mantra is repeated mentally, without at least mouthing it, it can be interrupted by extraneous thoughts.

Therefore, one should not place too much emphasis on how the mantra is said, as long as it is said for the designated time. This usually consists of a period between twenty minutes and a half hour, as mentioned earlier. If you wish, you may use a silent timer to signal when the meditation period is over. This is preferable to looking at a clock, which takes the mind off the meditation. You can also have someone else signal you when the time is up. After a while, however, you will automatically know when the period of meditation is over.

At first, you may allow the mind to wander freely while reciting the mantra. As long as you have an inner awareness that the words *Ribbono shel Olam* denote "Master of the Universe," the words themselves will pull your thoughts in a meaningful direction. No matter where the thoughts lead, there is no cause for concern. A Chasidic teaching says that any thought that enters the mind during meditation does so for a purpose.

It is also instructive to pay attention to the visual images you see while meditating with the eyes closed. As you become more advanced, these images become clearer and more vivid, and it becomes much easier to focus on them. Beyond that, as days pass, your control over these images improves dramatically during the meditative state. The vividness of these images can also become spectacular.

One must be careful, however, not to take these images too seriously. As one advances, the images become more explicit and can take the form of visions. The neophyte meditator may be tempted to place great significance on these visions, and think that he is actually experiencing prophecy or the like. It is therefore important to realize that any visions one may experience are not important and that undue emphasis should not be placed on them. Unless a person is extremely advanced, it is assumed that any visions he experiences are creations of the mind and nothing more.

In the Kabbalah literature, there are warnings even to advanced meditators not to give credence to visions. Even the most impressive visions can be spurious and come from the Other Side. Indeed, acting on the basis of images seen while in a meditative state is considered to be extremely dangerous and detrimental to one's spiritual development. Therefore, when a person experiences images or visions, they should be taken as aesthetic experiences and nothing more. At most, they should be taken as the first hints of a spiritual experience.

In general, bodily motion destroys concentration during mantra meditation and should be avoided. Some people, however, report that a slight, very slow swaying, perhaps a half inch in each direction, helps ease tension during the initial stages. If you find this helpful, you may use it.

At first, during meditation, you may allow the mind to wander freely or concentrate on the images you see in your mind's eye. However, as you become more advanced, you should begin to allow the words of the mantra to fill the mind completely, blanking out all sensation. This involves keeping all other thoughts out of the consciousness. All of your attention should be focused on the words of the mantra, leaving no room for any other thought.

Of course, until you become proficient in this discipline, extraneous thoughts will constantly try to push their way into the mind. You must then gently push them out, forcing your concentration back to the words of the mantra. This can sometimes take considerable effort, but it is the means through which one gains control of one's thoughts.

Some people find it easier to banish extraneous thoughts if they recite the mantra very slowly. As we shall see, slowness is also used in other types of meditation. At other times, however, it may be preferable to recite the mantra rapidly, sometimes even racing through the words. Here again, each individual must find his own pace.

After the meditation is over, remain in place for approximately five minutes, allowing the mind to absorb the effects of the meditation. You also need some time to "come back down" before returning to your daily routine. Again, you may wish to hum a soft melody during this period. It should be a time of intimate closeness with the Divine.

You may wish to use the moments following a meditation to have a short conversation with God. As mentioned earlier, Rabbi Nachman saw mantra meditation primarily as a means of preparing for such a divine conversation, which he saw as a higher type of meditation. In any case, one can feel very close to God after a meditation, and it is a good time to express that closeness. Whereas Eastern schools see mantra meditation as an end in itself, Jewish sources seem to indicate that it is more of a preparation for a deeper spiritual experience.

Some sources state that after meditating, one should smell fragrant spices or perfumes, so as to reinvolve oneself in the physical world. It is also prescribed that some light food be eaten shortly afterward, since through the blessing, the food can elevate the entire body.

Of course, meditating on the phrase *Ribbono shel Olam,* "Master of the Universe," has great value in its own right, and some people may be content to make it a lifetime practice. Others, however, may want to use it as a way to learn meditative techniques and recognize higher states of consciousness, and then go on to what are considered more advanced methods.

7 · Contemplation

Another simple type of meditation is contemplation. I have discussed this form of meditation in a previous chapter, in the context of *hitbonenuth*, but here I shall discuss it in further detail and in practical terms.

Contemplation consists in sitting and concentrating on an object, word, or idea, letting it fill the entire mind. This is an excellent introductory meditation, insofar as it does not require any background in meditation or any advanced knowledge of Hebrew or Judaism. The techniques are the same as those of mantra meditation, except that the experience is visual rather than verbal.

Simple contemplation consists of gazing at an object for a fixed period of time. As in all forms of meditation, one should be as comfortable as possible. There is no need to avoid blinking the eyes, since this can lead to discomfort. Rather, one should sit and gaze at the object of contemplation in the most relaxed manner possible.

The object of contemplation can be almost anything—a pretty stone, a leaf, a flower, or written material. Pictures, images, and statues, however, are to be avoided, since contemplating them is dangerously close to idolatry.

As in the case of mantra meditation, one should sit quietly in the meditation place, adjusting to the space. The meditation itself should take between twenty and thirty minutes. After the meditation, one should remain still for five to ten minutes, absorbing the effects of the exercise.

Visual contemplation is valuable in many respects. I have spoken earlier of visualization, in which one creates images in the mind's eye. Contemplation is a very good introduction to this practice. Once a person has learned to look at an object correctly, he can also learn to control his vision. Contemplation engraves the image in the mind's eye, and this image can then be conjured up even when the object is not present.

You can begin by using the object of contemplation as a focus for unstructured meditation. This would mean gazing at the object while letting the mind drift off in any direction it desires. The contemplation focuses the mind, but thought is left unbridled. You can think about how to restructure your life, about the meaning of life, or about any other subject important to you. Rather than being the goal of meditation, contemplation is an adjunct to a meaningful unstructured meditation.

As one becomes more advanced, one gradually learns how to fill the mind with the visual image of the object of contemplation, banishing all other thought. This is very much like mantra meditation, except that instead of filling the mind with a word or phrase, it is filled with an image. Extraneous thoughts are also shunted aside in a similar manner; whenever a thought enters the mind, it is gently pushed aside, leaving the entire attention fixed on the object of contemplation.

At first one must make a conscious effort to rid the mind of extraneous thoughts. However, after a while, the object of contemplation becomes the total center of one's focus, and everything else seems to vanish. The experience of looking at the object becomes highly intensified. It is as if there were nothing else in the entire world besides the meditator and the object of contemplation.

When one reaches this state, every detail of the object assumes an importance of its own. Thus, for example, if one were contemplating a leaf, every line and vein on it take on major significance. One would see structure and patterns to which the mind would normally be oblivious. Every detail would become deeply engraved in one's consciousness.

There is great leeway in what can be used as an object of meditation. If desired, a different object can be used at each session. This is of necessity true if the object of contemplation is something perishable, such as a leaf or a flower. However, when a different object is used each time, the effects are not cumulative.

It is therefore best to use the same object for a relatively long period of time. If possible the object should remain the same for thirty to forty days, long enough to habituate to it. Then, the experience of each session is reinforced, and each day's experience builds on that of the previous days.

It is important, however, to realize that the object of contemplation is merely an aid and not an end in itself. One must be extremely careful not to make the object of contemplation into an object of devotion, since to do so would border on idolatry. Even when one becomes aware of the Divine in the object, it may not be made into a venerated object or an object of devotion. Since this is always a danger, it is best to limit oneself to types of contemplation actually mentioned in classical Judaic literature.

People sometimes ask, if one can only do one type of meditation, whether one should begin with mantra meditation or with contemplation. To a large degree, this is a matter of personal preference. Some people are more verbal, while others are more visually oriented. For one who is verbal, mantra meditation will work more effectively, while one who is more visually oriented may find it easier to fill the mind with visual contemplation. Of course, if a person has a spiritual master who knows his soul and psyche, then the master can help him to make the decision.

However, both mantra meditation and contemplation are meant to develop different areas of the mind and spirit. Therefore, both are important. There are also important meditations that involve the senses of the body. For beginners, however, mantra meditation usually seems the simplest.

Some people find it valuable to combine mantra meditation with contemplation. If a person has learned to focus his mind through mantra meditation, then he can also use this method to enhance his contemplation. It is very easy to fill the mind with a visual image when one is in a higher state of consciousness from mantra meditation. In this sense, mantra meditation can be seen as an excellent introduction to contemplation.

Furthermore, as we have seen, the most universal Jewish mantra is the expression *Ribbono shel Olam*, "Master of the Universe." This mantra does not negate physical reality but focuses our attention on the physical universe and makes us aware of its Master. Thus, this mantra is an excellent way of relating the visible world to its Creator.

There is a vast difference between the English concept of universe and the Hebrew concept. In English, the word "universe" comes from the Latin *unus*, meaning "one," and *versum*, meaning "to turn." Hence, "universe" denotes that which is turned into one, or that which is combined into an integral whole. Thus, in the secular sense, the universe is seen as the main unifying factor in creation.

The Hebrew word for universe, on the other hand, is *olam*, which is derived from the root *alam*, meaning "to conceal." Therefore, in a Hebrew sense, the universe is seen as that which conceals the Divine. Thus, when one says *Ribbono shel Olam*, denoting "Master of the Universe," one is saying that concealed behind the universe, there is a Master. Thus, in repeating this mantra, one is making oneself aware of the hidden reality behind the visible one.

When a person uses the mantra *Ribbono shel Olam* together with contemplation on a physical object, he can actually begin to see the Divine hidden in the object. He can make the object of contemplation into a link between himself and God. The object becomes a channel through which he can experience the Divine.

Although any physical object can be used as the focus of meditation, several are mentioned specifically in Judaic literature, especially in the Kabbalah. Each of these has an important significance in its own right.

One type of meditation mentioned in the Zohar (1:1b, 2:231b) involves contemplating the stars. The Zohar provides a biblical source for this type of meditation, from the verse, "Lift your eyes on high, and see who created these, the One who brings out their host by number, He calls them all by name . . ." (Isa. 40:26). The verse is seen by the Zohar as prescribing a contemplation meditation with the stars as its object.

The Zohar notes that in the verse, there are two key Hebrew words, *MI*, meaning "who," and *ELeH*, meaning "these." When these two words are combined, the Hebrew letters (capitalized here) spell out *ELoHIM*, the Hebrew name for God. Thus, when one looks at the "these"—things in the ordinary mundane world—and asks "who?"—who is the author and basis of these things?—one finds God. The Zohar presents this in the context of the stars, but it is true of any object of contemplation.

People often gaze at the stars and feel a sense of awe and smallness in the face of the Infinite. But if one does it as a specific meditation, contemplating the stars and removing all other thought from the mind, the sense of awe and the feeling of God's presence in creation are greatly enhanced. One's focus goes beyond the stars, seeking what is beyond them—the "who" behind the "these"—and one becomes aware of their Creator.

A beginner may find it difficult to contemplate the stars in this manner without becoming overwhelmed by extraneous thoughts. Therefore, a mantra such as *Ribbono shel Olam* can be extremely useful. As it were, one is looking at the stars as *concealing* a greater and deeper truth, and the mind and soul probe and search to penetrate this mystery. When saying *Ribbono shel Olam*—"Lord of the Universe"—one is, as it were, calling to God in the depths of the heavens, seeking to find Him beyond the stars, beyond the very limits of time and space. This can bring a person to an overwhelmingly deep spiritual experience.

There are other ways in which a mantralike device can be combined with contemplation. Thus, for example, one may contemplate a flower and wish to gain a greater awareness of its beauty. Contemplation itself, of course, will greatly enhance awareness, but a beginner may find it difficult to maintain concentration. However, the contemplation can be combined with an exercise in which one repeats the word "beauty" over and over while looking at the flower. This serves to amplify one's sensitivity and sense of beauty, so that the flower will actually appear to radiate beauty. The result can be an extremely powerful aesthetic experience. If one then realizes that the source of beauty is the Divine in the flower, then this beauty can also become a link with the Divine.

Similarly, one can gaze at one's own hand and repeat the word "strength" over and over. When one does this, one can become uniquely aware of the strength in one's own hand. It is true that strength is normally an abstract quality, which one can be aware of but cannot see. However, in a meditative state, the strength of one's hand becomes not merely something of which one is aware in an abstract sense, but something that one can actually see. It is impossible to describe what strength looks like, but it actually becomes visible. This is very much like a synesthesia experience, discussed earlier, in which one can see unseeable things such as sounds or fragrances. Here, one can see abstract concepts as well.

Another type of contemplation mentioned in the Zohar involves a candle or oil lamp. Many meditative systems make use of a candle, but Judaic sources indicate a preference for a small lamp using olive oil and a linen wick. This would be like the great *menorah* candelabrum that stood in the Jerusalem Temple, which may have also been used as the object of contemplation. Olive oil has a particularly pure white flame that draws the gazer into its depths. Of course, if such a lamp is not available, a candle may be used instead, since the main thing is the flame.

The Zoharic literature (*Tikkunay ha-Zohar* 21:50a) teaches that in contemplating a flame, one should be aware of its five colors: white, yellow, red, black, and sky-blue. These are the colors that one should see when deeply contemplating the flame of a candle or oil lamp.

On an intellectual level, this is impossible to understand. When you simply look at a flame, you may see white, yellow, and red, since these are the natural colors of fire. Even the black may not be that difficult to understand, since it can be seen as the darkness around the flame. As we have seen, darkness itself plays an important role in the meditative experience.

However, the sky-blue color appears to present difficulty. There is no evidence whatever of this color in the flame of a candle or lamp. Furthermore, from the context of the Zoharic teaching, it appears that this color appears outside and beyond the black, which is the darkness around the flame.

However, elsewhere, the Zohar (3:33a) provides a hint as to the nature of this sky-blue color. The Zohar says that the blue that one sees around the flame represents the Divine Presence, *Shekhinah* in Hebrew.

In order to understand this, however, one must actually do a candle or lamp meditation. It should be done in an otherwise dark room, with the candle far enough from the wall so that it casts no light on it. Again, one uses the standard contemplation technique, allowing the flame to fill the entire mind. One becomes aware of the colors in the flame, the white, the yellow, and the red; each color and gradation of color is extremely significant. One is aware of the heat and energy radiating from the candle, and, as in the case of the hand's strength mentioned above, one reaches a level at which one can actually see these abstract energies.

The next step would be to concentrate on the darkness around the flame. When one contemplates the darkness of the room, it becomes a very profound, palpable darkness. One sees it as a velvety blackness that appears to radiate darkness. This may be analogous to the "black fire" or "lamp of darkness" discussed in Talmudic and Zoharic literature. In this sense, experiencing the darkness can be more profound than experiencing the light.

However, when one gets deeper into the meditation, one will begin to see a sky-blue field around the darkness. The blackness will extend for a certain distance around the candle, but around this will be an experience of pure sky-blue. It will be the most beautiful sky-blue color imaginable, like that of a summer sky over the Holy Land. The color will have an almost awesome beauty.

Of course, the blue color is not a physical reality; it is entirely a creation of the mind. But according to the Zohar, the blue sensation is a revelation of the spiritual. In a sense, it denotes that one is seeing the spiritual essence of the light that is radiating from the candle.

There are sources that indicate that in more advanced meditative techniques, it is possible actually to see visions in this blue field (see *Sefer Yetzirah* 1:12). Furthermore, in conjunction with the revelation at Sinai, when the Israelites had a vision of the Divine, they saw "under His feet like a brickwork of sapphire" (Exod. 24:10). Similarly, when the prophet Ezekiel saw the Throne of Glory, he described it as being the color of the sapphire (Ezek. 1:26). Thus, blue is always a color associated with vision and prophecy.

This type of candle meditation is important for a number of reasons. First, it gives us an experience of "black fire" and "radiating darkness," both of which are important concepts in Kabbalistic sources. As we shall see, "black fire" plays an important role in other types of Jewish meditation.

Second, in learning how to see the blue aura around the candle, one can learn how to see auras in general. An aura is a bluish field that appears around people and other objects. To see such an aura, one can begin by gazing at one's hand against a blank white wall or a clear blue sky. One will eventually see something like an area of color that somehow "feels" different than either the object or the background. This blurred area of color appears to extend outward from an eighth to a quarter of an inch from the object. At first it may be difficult to see, but with practice the aura becomes highly evident. Contemplation dramatically increases one's ability to see it.

In Kabbalistic sources, this aura is known as the *tzelem*. There were some spiritual masters, such as the Ari, who could determine the state of a person's spiritual health on the basis of the aura. Of course, reading auras is a subject that is beyond the scope of this book.

The color blue is also associated with the spiritual in other ways. One of the important commandments involves the tassels that were once worn on the corners of all garments. This survives today in the *tallith*, the tassled garment worn for prayer. In ancient times, one thread of the tassels would be dyed a bright sky-blue, using a dye made from the purpura snail (see Num. 15:38). Although it is no longer used, the blue was seen as highly significant.

Thus, the Talmud provides us with a contemplation meditation on the blue thread of the tassel. It says:

The tassel is blue;
The blue is the color of the sea;
The sea is the color of the sky;
And the sky is the color of the Throne of Glory.

Therefore, one may use the blue thread as the subject of a contemplation meditation. It can then fill the mind with this sky-blue color, so that nothing else exists in the world besides this blue. One then meditates on the association and sees the blue as the sea. Of course, since the blue dye comes from an aquatic creature, one is reaching back in this meditation to the source of the blue. But one also experiences the cool calmness of the sea and the serenity of its depths.

The next stage is to associate the blue of the sea with that of the sky. Now one's thoughts soar up to the heavens, higher and higher, up to the farthest reaches of the sky. Then one's thoughts penetrate the sky, and one approaches the Throne of Glory. Thus, contemplating the color blue is seen as bringing a person into the spiritual on an entirely different level. What is very signficant, however, is the fact that this type of contemplation meditation is described explicitly in the Talmud.

It is also significant that, in Kabbalah sources, this sapphire-blue color is also associated with the "third eye." One reason is that this color is seen not with the physical eyes, but with a mental or spiritual eye. In this blue, one can see visions that are invisible to the physical eyes.

There is another type of contemplation that is fairly straightforward and simple. This consists in contemplating God's most sacred name, the four-letter Tetragrammaton, YHVH (יהוה). This contemplation has a number of important advantages, the most obvious being that since it is God's most sacred name, it provides one with a direct link to the Divine.

One must realize that it is forbidden to pronounce this name in any form whatsoever. This is because it is the holiest of God's names, and it is linked to every spiritual level. But for this very reason, this name can be used as a ladder through which a person can link himself to the highest spiritual levels.

To use this method of contemplation, this name of God can be written on a card or sheet and placed where it can be seen easily. Then it can be used as an object of contemplation in the usual manner.

One may wish to enhance this contemplation with mantra meditation. Here again, the mantra *Ribbono shel Olam* can be very useful. One is then relating to God directly both through the mantra and through the visual contemplation.

For this type of contemplation to be most meaningful, one must have some idea of the meaning of the four letters of God's name. As I have said, the Tetragrammaton is spelled YHVH (יהוה). It therefore consists of the four Hebrew letters *yod* (י), *heh* (ה), *vav* (ו), and *heh* (ה). These four letters have a very special significance.

This name can be understood on the basis of an ancient Kabbalistic teaching. The teaching states that the four letters contain the mystery of charity.

According to this teaching, the first letter, *yod*, denotes the coin. The letter *yod* (י) is small and simple like a coin.

The second letter, *heh* (ה), denotes the hand that gives the coin. Every letter in the Hebrew alphabet also represents a number. Since *heh* is the fifth letter of the alphabet, it has a numerical value of five. The "five" of *heh* alludes to the five fingers of the hand.

The third letter, *vav* (ו), denotes the arm reaching out to give. This letter has the form of an arm. Furthermore, in Hebrew the word *vav* denotes a hook, and thus *vav* has the connotation of connection. Indeed, in Hebrew, the word for the conjunction "and" is represented by the letter *vav* prefixed to a word.

Finally, the fourth letter, the final *heh* (ה), is the hand of the beggar who accepts the coin.

This is the essence of charity on a mundane level. However, "charity" can also be understood on a divine scale. The greatest possible act of charity is that act through which God gives to us. The greatest charity that God gives is existence itself. We have no claim to existence and cannot demand that God give it to us as our right. Therefore, when He gives us existence, it is an act of charity. Since this "charity" is denoted by the Tetragrammaton, the four letters represent the mystery of the creative link between God and man.

Here again, the *yod* represents the "coin." But this time, the coin is not a piece of copper or silver, but existence itself. As the tenth letter of the Hebrew alphabet, *yod* has a numerical value of ten. Hence, according to the Kabbalists, it alludes to the Ten Sayings of Creation. The concept of the Ten Sayings is found even in the Talmud and is not necessarily a mystical teaching. In the account of creation in Genesis, the expression "And God said" occurs ten times; these are the Ten Sayings. These sayings represent the entire act of creation, and therefore represent the "coin" of existence that God gives us.

The *heh* of the name is then God's hand, which holds the existence He wishes to give us. The *vav* is His arm reaching out to us, to give us existence. Finally, the last *heh* of the name is our hand, which accepts this existence. Of course, God must give us even this hand. Thus, in a sense, God gives us the "hand" through which we receive existence from Him.

As one gazes at the four letters of the Tetragrammaton, one can actually see this.

One begins by contemplating the *yod* (י), which is the smallest letter of the Hebrew alphabet, almost like a dot. One contemplates the *yod* and sees it as the initial point of creation, the Ten Sayings that brought creation into existence out of nothingness.

One then contemplates the first *heh* (ה) of the name. This is the level of the Divine at which a vessel comes into existence to hold the abstract power of creation. One sees God holding the power of creation, so as to give it to us. The opening at the top of the *heh* is the channel from God, while the opening at the bottom is the channel to us below. The *heh* is thus seen both as a five-fingered hand (based on its numerical value) and as a channel for the forces of creation.

One then contemplates the *vav* (ו). Here one sees God's power reaching out to us, wanting to give.

The most important letter is the final *heh* (ה). This is our hand, into which we receive what God is ready to give us. This represents our ability to receive from God.

The connection between the *vav* and the *heh* is extremely important. This is the connection between the Giver and the receiver. Unless this connection is made, we cannot receive anything from God.

In the Talmud and the Kabbalah, the letters of the Hebrew alphabet are seen as having tremendous spiritual power. Speaking of Bezalel, the architect of the Tabernacle that the Israelites built right after the Exodus, the Talmud says, "Bezalel knew how to combine the letters through which heaven and earth were created." Since the world was created with Ten Sayings, and the sayings consist of letters, the letters are seen as the primary ingredients of creation. Thus, when one contemplates the Tetragrammaton, the letters serve as the means through which a person connects himself to God and the creative process.

There is another way of looking at the four letters of the Tetragrammaton. The first two letters, *yod* (י) and *heh* (ה), are seen as representing the masculine forces of creation. The last two letters, *vav* (ו) and *heh* (ה), represent the masculine and feminine forces of divine providence.

This is very closely related to the previous discussion. The first *yod* of the Tetragrammaton is seen as the "coin," the Ten Sayings of Creation. This is the "seed" of creation, the masculine element. This "seed" must be placed into the womb of creation, which is the *heh*, before it can be brought into fruition. The *heh* thus represents both a hand and a womb. Both have the connotation of holding, although the symbolism is different.

The last two letters of the name, *vav* and *heh*, represent the masculine and feminine powers of divine providence. Providence denotes the power through which God directs the world. Here, the *vav* represents the "seed" of providence, the initial impetus that comes from God. In a sense, it is God's "arm" of creation reaching out to direct the world He created. The final *heh* of the name is the hand with which we accept God's providence. This can also be seen as the womb that holds the forces of providence. The small opening on the top of the *heh* (ה) is the opening through which the "seed" enters, while the large opening at the bottom is where the "child" emerges.

Of course, the forces of creation can never be separated, since if they were, the world would cease to exist. The forces of providence, on the other hand can be separated, as when God turns His face away from the world. When the masculine and feminine forces of providence are separated, the *vav* in the name is separated from the final *heh*.

In this meditation on the Tetragrammaton, one can unite the *vav* and the final *heh*. In Kabbalah texts, this is known as a unification, *yichud* in Hebrew. It serves to open the person to the forces of providence and make him aware of divine guidance in his life. Since the *heh* is the hand through which we receive from God, uniting it with the *vav* makes a person more aware of the Divine Presence.

As one gazes at the name of God written on the card or parchment, the black of the writing becomes blacker, while the white of the card becomes whiter. Eventually, one perceives the name as being written with "black fire on white fire." It is significant to note that according to the Midrash the primeval Torah was written in this manner, as "black fire on white fire."

After one has been involved in this form of meditation for a period of time, the "fire" begins to burn the name of God into one's mind so that one can easily visualize it, even without the card. This involves the method of visualization, another important technique of Jewish meditation, which is the subject of the next chapter.

8 · Visualization

Earlier, I spoke about the images that one sees when the eyes are closed. An important discipline in meditation is learning how to control these images. When one has learned how to control them, one can also learn how to hold an image in the mind's eye. This technique is known as visualization.

A simple way to begin this discipline is to close your eyes and try to picture a letter of the alphabet, for example, the letter *A*. If you know the Hebrew alphabet, you can try to visualize the letter *alef* (**א**). Since there are Jewish meditations that use the letter *alef*, I shall use it as an example, although any other letter or figure could also be used.

To begin a visualization meditation, just close your eyes and relax, allowing the images in the mind's eye to settle down. If you have been practicing mantra meditation, you may want to use it as a relaxing mechanism. In any case, after a few minutes, the images in the visual field will become easier to control.

When the visual field is fairly calm, you can begin to try to visualize the *alef*. You may have an *alef* printed on a card and set the image of it in your mind. Then close your eyes and try to picture the *alef*. Try to see it with your eyes closed exactly as you saw it with your eyes open.

At first, this may be extremely difficult. The images that you see in your mind's eye are very difficult to control. If you have never done this before, it will be almost impossible the first time.

One important aid in visualization is the name of the object to be visualized. If you are trying to visualize the *alef*, you may repeat the word *alef* to yourself periodically. You may even wish to repeat the word over and over, as if it were a mantra. This not only relaxes the visual field, but locks the mind on to the *alef*. Repeating the word *alef* as a mantra will bring the letter into the mind's eye.

Another good aid is to initiate the visualization exercise with a contemplation meditation. If you wish to visualize the *alef*, first spend several days contemplating the letter written on a card approximately twenty minutes a day. This will serve to fix the image in the mind. It will then be much easier to fix the *alef* in the visual field with the eyes closed.

If you still encounter difficulty, the meditation session can be split between contemplation and visualization. Spend the first fifteen minutes of a half-hour session contemplating the *alef*, looking at it with your eyes open. Then, during the next fifteen minutes, you can try to visualize it with the eyes closed.

The ability to do this exercise varies from individual to individual. Some are able to do it the first time, while others have to work for weeks before they can visualize a letter. With patience and perseverance, however, it can be done by almost anyone.

Even after depicting the letter in the mind's eye, the average person will be able to hold the image only for several seconds. Then, like all such images, it will dissolve into other images. With time and practice, one eventually develops the ability to hold the image clearly and firmly in the mind's eye for extended periods. When this is accomplished, one has come a long way in gaining control over the mental processes.

The ability to hold an image in the mind's eye is discussed at length in the Kabbalah texts dealing with meditation. Thus, the *Sefer Yetzirah* refers to two processes in depicting the letters, "engraving" (*chakikah*) and "hewing" (*chatzivah*). Both processes are seen as important if one is going to depict the letters. As discussed in the previous chapter, the Hebrew letters are seen as channels of the forces of creation, and as such they can be used as a powerful means of drawing down spiritual energy. However, "engraving" and "hewing" are useful also for less esoteric forms of meditation.

The term "engraving" denotes fixing an image in the mind's eye so that it does not waver or move. No matter what other images may arise in the field of vision, the engraved image remains there, as if the image were actually engraved in the mind. Once a person has accomplished this, he can usually depict the desired image as soon as he begins his meditation, almost as a reflex.

However, even when the image is clear and steady—"engraved" in the mind, as it were—it is usually surrounded by other images. The next step is to isolate the image. Thus, for example, if one were visualizing the letter *alef*, one would attempt to isolate it and rid the mind's eye of all other imagery. This is known as "hewing," or *chatzivah*. The analogy is to hewing out a stone from the surrounding rock. The process consists in designating the desired stone and then hewing away the extraneous stone. One does the same thing in the mind, hewing away all extraneous imagery surrounding the desired form. All that is left is the image one desires.

There are a number of ways of "hewing" away surrounding imagery. One way is to replace all the mental images other than the *alef* with pure white. First focus on the *alef*, allowing it to fill the mind. Then gradually hew away the images around the *alef*, replacing them with white fire. Imagine the white fire burning away the other images. Begin with a small spot of white fire at the top of the *alef*, using it to burn away a small spot of imagery. Let the white fire expand, burning away larger and larger areas. As it moves around the *alef*, burning away images on all sides. Finally, one sees the *alef* alone, written in black fire on white fire.

In general, a visualization technique such as this is very valuable and can be used in other forms of Jewish meditation. Thus, many classical Kabbalah texts speak about *yichudim* or "unifications," which I discussed briefly in the previous chapter. For the most part, the meditational method of *yichudim* involves imaging various names of God and then manipulating the letters. In general, the method of *yichudim* is highly advanced and requires some knowledge of Kabbalah.*

A good introduction to the method of *yichudim* involves visualizing the Tetragrammaton, YHVH (יהוה). This is similar to the technique of contemplating the Tetragrammaton, described in the previous chapter, but here it is done without any external aid. Significantly, an exercise that entails visualizing the Tetragrammaton is mentioned in the *Shulchan Arukh*, the standard code of Jewish law. It is also an introduction to a number of other, more advanced techniques discussed in the Kabbalah.

By visualizing God's name, one can attain a tremendous feeling of closeness to God. One actually feels the presence of God and experiences a deep sense of awe in the presence. A number of classical Judaic sources find an allusion to such visualization in the verse "I have placed YHVH before me at all times" (Ps. 16:8). This type of visualization is also useful during worship and prayer.

Here, too, you can use contemplation as an introduction to visualization. If you find it difficult to visualize the Tetragrammaton, spend a number of days contemplating the name written on a sheet or card. You can spend the first half of a session contemplating the written name and the other half visualizing it with the eyes closed. Eventually, you will be able to visualize it without using the card at all.

Once you become adept at visualizing the name, you can use it for the simple *yichud* discussed in the last chapter. As discussed there, the *vav*(ו) and final *heh* (ה) of the name are the masculine and feminine forces of providence. When the *vav* and *heh* are separated, there is no connection between God and the world below other than His creative energy. Therefore, like a man and woman in love, the *vav* and *heh* yearn and long to be united, to bring God's power to the lower world. When the *vav* and *heh* are united, God's presence becomes palpable and one can have a very strong experience of the Divine.

---

*In my book *Meditation and Kabbalah*, a number of important *yichudim* are presented in their entirety.

One accomplishes this *yichud* by visualizing the divine name, YHVH (יהוה). One focuses on the *vav* and *heh*, making oneself aware of the longing and yearning of these two letters to unite. When the longing between the two letters becomes unbearable, they finally unite, and a spiritual flood is released. One feels this as a torrent of divine energy flowing through the body and mind. One is bathed in the spiritual experience and overwhelmed by it, totally opened up, like a vessel for the divine.

Once proficiency in visualization is achieved, there are more advanced methods that one can learn. One such method, mentioned in the Kabbalistic sources, is to imagine the sky opening up and to depict oneself ascending into the spiritual realm. One rises through the seven firmaments, one by one, until one reaches the highest heaven. On this level, one depicts in one's mind a huge white curtain, infinite in size, filling the entire mind. Written on this white curtain, one visualizes the Tetragrammaton.

The black of the letters and the white of the curtain become intensified, until the letters appear to be black fire on white fire. Gradually, the letters of the Tetragrammaton expand, until they appear to be huge mountains of black fire. When the four letters fill the mind completely, one is, as it were, swallowed up in God's name.

On a still more advanced level, the letters appear to be not merely written on the curtain, but solid objects, with both dimension and texture. One can see oneself actually entering into the letters, surrounded by their essence on all sides.

Finally, one can reach the level where one sees the letters as living entities, as if each letter were an angelic being. One becomes uniquely aware of the life force and spiritual energy in each letter, of the significance of the letters and of the flow of energy between one letter and the next. One becomes aware of the unification of the Giver with the receiver and of the ultimate male and female elements of creation.

These last methods can bring a person to very high spiritual levels and should not be taken lightly. The original sources state that before attempting any of these more advanced methods, one should spend the entire day in preparation, reciting the Psalms and studying Torah. Before beginning the meditation, one should immerse oneself in a *mikveh* (ritual bath) or any other natural body of water to cleanse oneself both physically and spiritually. Some sources also indicate that one should dress totally in white for these advanced meditations.

This type of visualization can be dangerous and should not be attempted without an experienced spiritual master or a meditation partner. The Baal Shem Tov recommends that one have a partner for any type of advanced meditation. Then, if necessary, one partner can bring the other back to the real world.

Visualization is valuable for another reason. In deeper forms of meditation, one often sees visions. As I discussed earlier, these visions should not be taken too seriously. Unless a person is very advanced and working under the tutelage of an experienced master, these visions are almost certain to be spurious. It is therefore recommended that when any visions appear, they be banished from the mind. If one learns to control one's visualization, then this is fairly easy. Some sources recommend that visions, when they occur, should be banished from the mind and replaced with the Tetragrammaton.

When one learns how to control the imagery in the mind's eye, there is much less danger that spurious visions will appear. One's meditation is then pure and undisturbed by low-level side effects.

9·Nothingness

Meditation on nothingness is a topic upon which I have touched briefly in an earlier chapter. Actually, this is a very advanced type of meditation and not for beginners. It is not recommended for practice without the guidance of a spiritual master and should never be practiced alone. I shall discuss it here because this technique is closely related to visualization methods and is important for understanding a number of other areas in Jewish meditation and mysticism.

Once proficiency has been achieved in visualization techniques, it is possible to attempt to visualize pure nothingness. Nothingness has no counterpart in the real world, so one must be able to create a perception of it in the mind. It is a useful technique to attain closeness to God and to achieve a realization of the self.

As in the case of other advanced techniques, this can be extremely dangerous. The reason why it should never be practiced alone is that one can get "swallowed up" in the nothingness of the meditation and not be able to return. Therefore, one should always have a partner or a spiritual master available to bring one back to objective reality.

Before we can begin to discuss this type of meditation, we must have an idea of what nothingness looks like. When one first thinks of nothingness, one may image it as being like the blackness of empty space. The interplanetary void may seem as close to nothingness as a person can imagine. If one is expert in visualization, it is fairly easy to visualize empty space and pure empty blackness. This indeed may be a first step toward visualizing nothingness, but it is not nothingness. Space is space, and blackness is blackness—neither is nothingness.

A next step in attempting to visualize nothingness would be to attempt to visualize pure, transparent, empty space, without any background color. One can imagine oneself looking into a pure, colorless, transparent crystal, with the transparency extending to infinity. According to some commentaries, this is the connotation of the "brickwork of sapphire" that the Israelites saw under God's feet (Exod. 24:10). These commentaries translate the Hebrew expression *livenath ha-sappir* as "transparency of crystal" rather than "brickwork of sapphire." They say that it is related to the meditation in which one images pure transparence without any color. One images first the transparency of crystal and then the transparency of pure colorless empty space.

One way to do this is to image the air in front of you. It is, of course, perfectly transparent, and therefore you cannot see it. Instead you see what is at the other end of the room. Using the "hewing" technique described in the previous chapter, you should be able to rid yourself of the image of the other end of the room; then you will have a pure image of the transparent air around you. It will be pure transparence, with no form or color.

Years ago, I found this to be a very helpful technique for experiencing the presence of God. It is an important teaching of Judaism that God is omnipresent, totally filling all creation. The clearest statement of this is the verse "The whole world is filled with His glory" (Isa. 6:3). God fills all creation and is even present in the air around us. I would therefore contemplate the air around me and imagine it filled with God's presence. This would bring a very great feeling of God's closeness.

Now, although this technique involves imaging the transparent empty space, what is imaged is still space; it is not nothingness.

So what does nothingness look like?

It is taught that nothing is what you see behind your head. Of course, sight does not extend behind the head. Therefore, what you see behind the head is *nothing*. In other words, you see nothingness.

This teaching can be used as a contemplation. Attempt to contemplate what you see behind your head. You realize that it is nothing, but with practice, you will be able to make it into an object of contemplation. This is a powerful technique to gain a conception of pure nothingness.

In the Bible, it appears that this or a similar technique was used as a precursor of prophecy. There are a number of references to voices and prophecy seeming to come from behind. Thus, Ezekiel said, "I heard behind me a loud voice proclaiming, 'Blessed be God's glory from His place' " (Ezek. 3:12). Likewise, regarding a certain degree of revelation, the prophet said, "Your ears shall hear a voice behind you" (Isa. 30:21). This might indicate that by meditating on the nothingness seen behind the head, one opens oneself up to the experience of prophecy.

Other sources, however, indicate that instead of contemplating what one sees behind the head, one should contemplate what one sees inside the head. This is a method discussed by Rabbi Abraham Abulafia, one of the most important writers on Kabbalistic meditation. Of course, what one sees inside the head is also nothingness, so the experience is essentially the same.

To learn how to visualize nothingness properly can take years. It is not an easy discipline. However, once one has a good depiction of nothingness, one can use it as a powerful visualization technique. Of all the images one can visualize, the purest is a vision of nothingness.

Visualizing nothingness is also a technique used in the most advanced meditational exercises. If one visualizes nothingness and at the same time clears the mind of thought, the mind becomes a total blank. The mind is then at its most sensitive, open to even the most ethereal experiences. This is therefore an important technique for experiencing the spiritual.

This can sometimes be a traumatic experience. When one locks the mind on to a visualization of nothingness and clears the consciousness of all other thought, the mind becomes so sensitive that even the slightest sensation can be overwhelming. It is like turning up a radio to full volume, so that the softest voice becomes a roar. On the other hand, it is only at full volume that the weakest signals can be heard.

At this level, even the random thoughts that tug at the corner of the mind are felt as mental earthquakes. Before one can proceed, one must dampen all thought completely. Finally, when all thought is quieted, one can have an experience of the spiritual. This involves a deep feeling of awe, shame, and humility.

Some Kabbalists teach that this is the mystery of Ezekiel's vision. At the very beginning of his vision, the prophet says, "I looked, and saw a storm wind coming from the north, a great cloud, and flashing fire . . . " (Ezek. 1:4). The Zohar teaches that the wind, the cloud, and the fire are the three barriers through which a prophet must pass before he enters the realm of the Divine.

The first thing that Ezekiel experienced was "a storm wind." There is a double meaning here, however, since the Hebrew word for wind is *ruach*, which also means "spirit." Therefore, what Ezekiel saw can also be translated as "a stormy spirit." The stormy spirit relates to the first experience mentioned earlier. When there is literally nothing in the mind, all the natural agitations of the mind are greatly intensified. This is the barrier of the "storm wind" through which the prophet must pass.

The second barrier the prophet encounters is "a great cloud." This is the muffling and restriction of all thought, an opaqueness of the mind, in which nothing can be seen or experienced. It is a barrier that can easily discourage the prophet if he does not have the will to proceed further. As he is trying to ascend, he faces a cloud barrier beyond which he cannot see and which he must strive to overcome.

The final barrier is the "flashing fire." This is the sense of awe, shame, and dread that the prophet experiences when he first breaks into the spiritual realm. Throughout the Bible, fire is a metaphor for shame and dread. Fire burns and hence is an overabundance of sensation—a sensation so intense that it cannot be tolerated. Thus, while the cloud is the obliteration of sensation, the fire is the opposite, the overabundance of sensation. The cloud also shows the prophet that one who is unworthy will not see anything, while the fire demonstrates that such a person may be in danger as well.

This is the manner in which meditation on nothingness opens the door to prophecy. It can also be used to get in touch with the innermost self. This, of course, raises the question, What is the nature of the self?

Normally, when a person thinks of himself, the first thing he thinks of is his body. It is almost a reflex action. Ask a person to point to himself, and he will almost inevitably point to his chest. Perhaps, if he is more perceptive, he will point to his head, the seat of his brain, seeing the mind as being more representative of the self than the body.

The Kabbalists point out that the body is not the self. Since I can speak of "*my* body," the body cannot be "me." The body is "mine"—something associated with the me; but the ultimate me is something much more profound than the body. Using the same argument, I can also speak of "*my* mind." Indeed, I speak of "my mind" just as I speak of "my body." This would imply that just as the body is not the real me, the mind is also not the real me. Carrying the argument a step further, I can even speak of "*my* soul." This would imply that even the soul is not the real me.

This being the case, the question of selfhood becomes very difficult indeed. What is the real me? A hint to the answer can be found in the Hebrew word for "I," *ani* (אֲנִי). It is significant to note that if the letters of *ani* are rearranged, they spell the word *ayn* or *ayin* (אַיִן), which denotes nothingness. This would seem to imply that the real "me" is the nothingness within me.

This can be understood in a fairly straightforward manner. The real me is my sense of volition. It is the intangible will that impels me to do whatever I decide to do. Even if I think, I must first will myself to think. In that sense, will is even higher than thought. It is obvious that it is the "I" that tells my mind to think.

However, the fact that I must will myself to think implies that the source of my will is on a level that is beyond thought. It is therefore impossible for me to imagine the source of my will, and there is no category in my conscious mind into which it will fit. Therefore, when I try to imagine the source of my will, the real "me," all I can depict is nothingness.

This can also be understood in another manner. Earlier I mentioned that there are three things that appear to be identifiable with the self: body, mind, and soul. As I noted, neither the body, the mind, nor the soul is the self. However, in another sense, the self is a combination of body, mind, and soul. The three together appear to define the self.

However, this has an important ramification. If body is not the self, and mind is not the self, and soul is not the self, but the combination of the three is, then the definition of the self is still an enigma. It would seem that it is possible to remove the body, remove the mind, and remove the soul, and still have some spark of the self. But when body, mind, and soul are removed, all that remains is nothingness. Again it appears that the self is nothingness.

It is not nothingness because of lack of existence. Rather, it is nothingness because of the lack of a category in the mind in which to place it. It is very much like the situation of what one sees behind one's head. One sees nothingness, not because there isn't anything there, but because one does not have eyes behind the head to see with. Where there is no sense organ, or no category in the mind, to grasp certain information, then that information is perceived as nothingness. If there is no other information competing with it, then it is an experience of pure nothingness.

This can also be understood in a deeper manner. If the most basic ingredient of self is will, then this must also be connected to the divine will. In this sense, a person's will comes from the spark of the Divine in the person. Therefore, when a person visualizes nothingness, he is, to some degree, in touch with the Divine within himself.

This can be understood on the basis of Kabbalistic teachings that the highest spiritual levels can be understood only in terms of nothingness. This may seem difficult to understand. To comprehend it, one must understand how Judaism in general, and the Kabbalists in particular, view God.

People often say that "God is spirit" or that "God is power" or that "God is love." But the fact is that none of these sentences is true. Actually, the sentence "God is . . ." is a statement that cannot be completed. To complete the sentence would be to place God in the same category as something else. If one understands the true nature of God, then this is impossible.

This truth is derived from the very basic Jewish teaching that God is the creator of *all things*. This has very important implications. For one, it means that even concepts as basic as will or mind are creations of God. Indeed, the Zohar explicitly states that God does not have will or mind in any anthropomorphic sense. Rather, in order to use will and mind to create the world, God first had to create these concepts. To say otherwise would be to imply that will and mind are coequal with God, which, again, is impossible.

Even logic itself must be seen as something created by God. Were this not so, and if we were to insist that God be bound by logic, then we would have to say that logic is higher than God, or more fundamental. Again, if we look at God as the creator of all things, then God must also be the creator of logic. This has important ramifications: if one discovers paradoxes in relation to God, it is not a problem. Paradoxes are merely ideas that transcend logic, and since God is the creator of logic, He can use it as He desires, but He is not bound by it. Of course, it is taught that God bound Himself by logic when He created the world, but this was a voluntary act, and not something intrinsic.

The fact that God created every category means that anything for which a word exists in the human language must of necessity denote something created by God. Even the word "God" itself denotes our conception of Him, and not His true essence. Since everything conceivable—including any category of thought that the mind can imagine—was created by God, there is nothing conceivable that can be associated with Him.

Let us say that I want to think about God. There is, however, no category in my mind in which I can place Him. Therefore, trying to depict God is like trying to see without eyes. When I try to see where there are no eyes, all I see is nothing. Similarly, when I try to think about God, all that my mind can depict is nothing.

The Zoharic literature expresses this by declaring to God, "No thought can grasp You at all." Rabbi Shneur Zalman of Lyady (1745–1813), one of the greatest Jewish mystics, notes that the Zohar uses the expression for "grasp" that is usually associated with a physical object. He explains, "Just as a hand cannot grasp thought, so the mind cannot grasp God." Our physical senses cannot grasp or detect thought and therefore experience it as nothing. The same is true of the way the mind experiences God.

Hence, the closest one can come to thinking about God is to depict nothingness and to realize that behind it is God. It is for this reason that nothingness meditation was seen as a means of drawing close to God.

This is not to say that we cannot speak about God at all. As the major Jewish philosophers point out, statements we make about God are either "attributes of action," stating what God *does,* or "negative attributes," saying what God *is not.* We may say that God is good, kind, loving, and omnipotent. However, these are all descriptions of what God does and how He acts, but not what He *is.*

It is important to realize that although we cannot speak *about* God, it is very easy to speak *to* God. Indeed, this is the subject of the following chapters.

When a person imagines nothingness, he should realize that this is the closest that it is possible to come to imagining God. Most certainly, this does not mean that God is nothingness. In every possible way, God is more real than anything else that exists. However, it means that since there is nothing in the human mind that can relate to God as He actually is, nothingness is the closest thing to a perception of God that we can obtain. When a person depicts nothingness, he must realize that behind the nothingness is God.

There is a method to image this. The technique consists in imaging the four letters of the Tetragrammaton as in chapter 8. However, when one "hews" away the surrounding imagery, instead of replacing it with "white fire," one replaces it with nothingness. One begins by imaging a small area of nothingness at the edge of the *yod*. This area of nothingness is expanded until it totally surrounds the four letters. The first few times that one attempts this, the letters may seem to be surrounded by transparent space. With practice, one can actually make the letters seem to be surrounded by nothingness.

If the letters are suspended in nothingness, there will appear to be nothing around them. In essence, the letters will fill the entire field of vision. Still, the letters are not warped or distorted in any way; rather, the space between them and around them is filled with nothingness. Of course, it is impossible to imagine this unless one has actually experienced it. Like panoscopic vision or synesthesia, it is something that cannot be described.

Another, even more advanced technique is to see the letters of the Tetragrammaton behind the nothingness. Then the letters are, as it were, hidden by nothingness, just as God Himself is. In a sense, this is similar to panoscopic vision. One "sees" nothingness, but one is simultaneously looking behind it, where one "sees" the letters of the Divine Name.

All of these techniques are described or alluded to in the Kabbalah literature. However, let me repeat that the techniques described in this chapter are all highly advanced and should not be attempted without expert guidance and considerable experience in meditational techniques.

10·Conversing with God

In the previous chapter, I discussed meditative techniques that are both highly advanced and potentially dangerous for a beginner. The technique that I shall discuss in this chapter, on the other hand, is very simple and is considered among the safest. Still, many people feel that it is one of the most powerful of all the Jewish meditative techniques.

Earlier, I spoke about how difficult it is to speak—or even to think—about God. God is totally ineffable, beyond the realms of thought and speech. Yet, as difficult as it is to speak *about* God, it is relatively easy to speak *to* Him. What person has not at some point in life prayed to God in his own words? If one is a believer, it is a natural reflex in times of trouble or distress to direct one's words toward God. When a loved one is ill or when one faces something unfaceable, one's thoughts and prayers automatically flow toward the Supreme Being. Prayer is a cry from the depths of the heart, from the ground of one's being, and communication is simple and direct.

Children naturally tend to pray to God. A child who is lonely or hurt will automatically call out to his Father in heaven. A child who has never been taught to pray may begin to do so on his own. It is as if there were a built-in instinct that leads us to call beyond the realm of the physical when we are in dire need.

It seems that, in general, Jews pray spontaneously less than non-Jews, at least nowadays. There seems to be a feeling that Jewish prayer must be in Hebrew, in a prescribed manner, with a predetermined wording. Many Jews are surprised to learn that there is an unbroken tradition of spontaneous prayer in the Jewish religion. If we look at the spectrum of Jewish literature, we find numerous references to spontaneous personal prayer. Many great Jewish leaders considered their own prayers to be very important to their spiritual development. And in Europe, it was the most natural thing in the world for Jews to cry out to God in their native Yiddish.

Although many sources discuss spontaneous prayer, one Jewish leader gave it a central role in his teachings: Rabbi Nachman of Bratslav. Rabbi Nachman was a great-grandson of the Baal Shem Tov, founder of the Chasidic movement. The Baal Shem taught that every individual could attain a strong personal relationship with God. Rabbi Nachman expanded this concept, teaching that the most powerful method to attain such a relationship with God is personal prayer in one's own native language.

This, of course, was not meant to downgrade the importance of the formal system of worship, which forms the Jew's daily order of devotion. The prescribed worship service is of paramount importance in Judaism. However, worship services can at times become dry and sterile. One's own personal prayers, on the other hand, are always connected to the wellsprings of the heart.

How does a person begin to speak to God? In times of crisis or trouble, it is almost automatic. There is a need to call out to someone, and one knows that God is always there. When our lives are on an even keel, on the other hand, it is not as easy. When everything is going our way, what is there to discuss with God? How does one begin a conversation? Sometimes, it is almost embarrassing.

It is very much like being away from a parent or a close friend for a long time. In times of crisis, it is easy to renew contact since the crisis itself serves as a point of departure. Similarly, when there are special occasions, it is easy to pick up the phone and say hello. This is why relatives often see one another only at weddings and funerals. Such occasions serve as an excuse to get together after prolonged absence.

To pick up the phone and, without any excuse, call a friend you have not spoken to in years is not a very easy thing to do. How does one justify the sudden, unexpected call? And perhaps most important of all, how does one justify not having made contact for the long period before the call?

For very much the same reason, it is difficult for some people to begin a conversation with God. How does one start such a conversation? And what does one say?

If you need an excuse, you can use this book. Tell God, "I just read this book about having conversations with God. I felt it was time I did it."

Another problem that people encounter when attempting to speak to God is that they feel inadequate. They are aware that God knows their shortcomings and sins, and they feel ashamed in His presence. Others may feel that their lives as Jews are not what they should be and that they cannot approach God as a Jew.

Even if one felt comfortable morally and religiously (and who really does?), there is a basic awe and feeling of inadequacy that everyone feels when trying to speak to God. It is told that the great Chasidic leader Rabbi Zusia of Hanipoli (c. 1720–1800) once came late to synagogue. When he was asked what happened, he replied that when he woke up in the morning, he began the usual prayer, "I give thanks before You . . ." (*Modeh ani lefanekha*). He said the first three words and could go no further. He explained, "I became suddenly aware of who the 'I' was, and who the 'You' was. I was struck speechless and could not continue."

All this adds up to the fact that many people consider it extremely difficult to initiate a conversation with God. Rabbi Nachman speaks about this at considerable length.

It is significant that Rabbi Nachman refers to this practice of speaking to God, not as prayer, but as meditation. It appears that the line between prayer and meditation here is a very fine one, but there is an important difference. When a person speaks to God spontaneously, whenever he feels impelled to do so, then it is prayer. When a person makes it a fixed practice and spends a definite time each day conversing with God, then it is meditation. As we have discussed earlier, meditation is thinking in a controlled manner. If this thinking consists in a conversation with God, it is no less a meditative experience.

In this context, Rabbi Nachman prescribes making a commitment to spending a fixed amount of time each day speaking to God. The amount of time he prescribes is approximately an hour every evening. In our fast-moving modern society, many find twenty to thirty minutes a more comfortable period for such conversation. The main thing is that it be for a fixed period of time and that it be practiced every day without fail.

The most difficult thing is to begin. Rabbi Nachman advises sitting down in the place where you meditate and saying to yourself, "For the next twenty mintes, I will be alone with God." This in itself is significant, since it is like the beginning of a "visit." Even if there is nothing to say, it is a valid experience since you are spending time alone with God, aware of His presence. If you sit long enough, says Rabbi Nachman, you will eventually find something to say.

If you have difficulty in beginning the conversation, Rabbi Nachman advises repeating the phrase "Master of the Universe" over and over. This can comprise the entire conversation. When you say these words, be aware that you are calling out to God. Eventually, your thoughts will open up, and you will find other ways of expressing yourself.

Of course, "Master of the Universe" is nothing other than *Ribbono shel Olam*, a phrase that I discussed earlier as a Jewish mantra. Here we see that it can also be used to call out to God in a most basic way, to establish communication.

If you still cannot begin speaking with God, Rabbi Nachman suggests making this difficulty itself the point of conversation. Tell God how much you would like to speak to Him. Explain to Him that it is hard for you to find something to say. Ask God to help you find words with which to address Him. Discuss the problem with Him as you would with a good friend. Once the conversation has begun, it is usually easy to continue.

Another point of departure can be the feeling of alienation and distance from God. You can initiate a conversation by asking God to bring you closer to Him. Tell him how far you feel from Him and how much closer you would like to be. Ask Him to help you find such closeness.

The conversation does not have to vary. One can speak to God about the same thing day after day, week after week. Obviously, it is impossible to bore God. Since this is a meditation, the regular habit of holding a conversation is as important as its content. If you are asking God to help you speak to Him, or to draw you closer, this exercise will help you develop your ability to hold more extensive conversations with God.

You can repeat the same sentence or phrase as often as you wish. Any significant sentence can be the point of the entire meditation. You can change the phrase or sentence that you are using at any time. Eventually, you will develop enough flexibility to express your thoughts to God freely.

In any case, just as with everything else, practice helps, and one can become proficient in holding conversations with the Infinite Being. Once you learn how to converse with God with ease, you can speak in a quiet, hushed voice, making yourself more and more aware of the One to whom you are speaking. As you converse, you will become increasingly aware of God's presence. At this point, the conversation with God becomes an awesome experience.

As the conversation becomes easier and more relaxed, the experience deepens. It becomes a powerful meditative technique, which can easily bring one to higher states of consciousness. In these states of consciousness, God's presence becomes almost palpable.

The question arises as to what advantage this method has over such other methods as mantra meditation or contemplation. Since this is an inner-directed meditation, it has some important advantages.

One of the purposes of meditation is to help banish the ego. This is often difficult in the modern world. Furthermore, in the high-pressure world of our everyday lives, a person must have a strong sense of self and purpose in order not to be trampled. For many people, a meditative regimen that weakens the ego and sense of self may be counterproductive. One may find one's goals in meditation diametrically opposed to one's ambitions and aspirations in the world.

The method of conversing with God does not have this drawback. It is true that, like other forms of meditation, this method can help a person overcome the ego. Nevertheless, this is a method that replaces the ego with something stronger. In speaking to God, a person can gain a view of himself from a different perspective and begin to see himself as a branch of the Divine. This type of meditation makes one, as it were, partners with the Divine. Thus, for example, if one has discussed future plans with God and still feels good about them, one's resolution and feeling of purpose are all the stronger.

Of course, this can have dangers in the opposite direction. If a person does not nullify his ego sufficiently, he can become so bullheaded and obstinate that people cannot deal with him. Nothing is so distasteful as a person who acts as if he has a direct line to God. Therefore, the goal is to attain and maintain a balance.

Besides strengthening one's resolve, conversing with God can also help one to find direction in life. I have discussed this earlier, when I spoke about a meditation concerned with rearranging one's life. Here again, by conversing with God, a person can see himself from a God's-eye view, as it were. He can then determine if the type of life he is leading is one that is worthy from God's point of view. If it is not, meditation will help him find ways of improving it.

It is significant that the Hebrew verb for praying is *hitpalel*. Hebrew linguists note that this is the reflexive of the word *palel*, meaning "to judge." Therefore, *hitpalel* means to judge oneself.

This is not difficult to understand in the context of our discussion. When a person speaks to God, he is able to see himself from a God's-eye view and he is judging himself in the deepest sense possible. He is looking at his most profound aspirations in the mirror of his prayer and judging whether or not they are worthy.

Little by little, the person can also purge himself of any encumbrances to prayer.

Actually, this is like a type of therapy. In many ways, speaking to God is like speaking to a therapist. What, then, is the difference between this method of prayer-meditation and psychotherapy?

First, it is true that both psychotherapy and meditation can help a person direct his life more effectively. In psychotherapy, however, the answer comes from without, while in prayer-meditation, the answer comes from within. If the person is basically healthy, his answers will reflect his own values and aspirations much more truly than if they are filtered through the eyes of a therapist who may have an entirely different value system. Prayer-meditation may also spur a person to learn more about life and its meaning from external sources, so that help can also come from without.

Furthermore, psychotherapy deals only with the mundane dimensions of man, and not with his spiritual dimensions. Prayer-meditation, on the other hand, deals primarily with the spiritual dimension. Psychotherapy is primarily a way of working out problems, while meditation is a method of enhancing the spiritual dimensions of life.

There are many ways in which prayer-meditation can be very much like self-therapy, and therefore, it has all the dangers inherent therein. As in therapy, a person can uncover deep, unresolved problems that can cause great pain and suffering if they are not worked out. In psychotherapy, one has the therapist to help if the situation becomes too difficult. If one is using meditation as self-therapy, on the other hand, one can get oneself into a psychological cul-de-sac and not be able to escape.

Therefore, if you find yourself using prayer-meditation as a form of self-therapy, it is very important that you have a guide who understands exactly what is happening. Without such a guide, the results can be more negative than positive. The guide should be someone who is well adjusted and psychologically strong, with extensive successful experience in guiding neophyte meditators. The guide's advice should help the meditator find a proper balance in his or her life.

11 · The Way of Prayer

One of my students, a psychiatrist-healer, once told me that when he began his involvement in spiritual practices, he used to rush through the morning service so that he would have time to meditate. This went on for a few months. Then, in one of our classes, we discussed how the worship service itself was originally designed to be meditative exercise and how it could be used as such. After this, he told me, instead of rushing through the morning service, he used the service itself as his daily meditation.

Many Jews are still uncomfortable with meditation. They feel that it is something from another culture, tacked onto Judaism. Although many traditional sources discuss Jewish meditation, after a century of neglect, many Jews find the notion difficult to accept. Even the word "meditation" has an alien ring to it, as if it were something borrowed from another world.

On the other hand, the most accepted manner for a Jew to relate to God is through the daily services. An observant Jew worships (or *davens*) three times a day. In most communities, the synagogues hold daily services. Of course, in Orthodox circles, daily prayer is considered an important part of the daily regimen.

The three daily services are the morning service, known as *shacharith;* the afternoon service, known as *minchah;* and the evening service, known as *maariv* or *arevith*. The service on the Sabbath and festivals is essentially the same, except that a fourth additional, or *musaf*, service is added in the morning after the Torah is read.

The focus of each of these services is the Amidah, which literally means "that which involves standing." The Amidah is a silent prayer that must be said while one is standing. On weekdays, it originally consisted of eighteen prayers and petitions, and is therefore also referred to as the Shemoneh Esreh, which literally means "The Eighteen." In the first century, a nineteenth prayer was added, making this appellation not strictly accurate.

The Amidah can be found in any standard Jewish prayer book. Of the eighteen sections, the first three and last three are always essentially the same, both on weekdays and on the Sabbath and Holy Days. On the Sabbath and Holy Days, however, the middle twelve (or thirteen) prayers are replaced with a single section relating to the Sabbath or festival.

The most important part of the Amidah, especially from a meditative point of view, is the opening paragraph. This paragraph consists of a short prayer that establishes the worshiper's basic relationship to God. This paragraph always forms the beginning of the Amidah, whether on weekdays or on Sabbaths or festivals.

In order to use this section of the Amidah as a meditation, one must memorize it. It is best to do so in the original Hebrew, since the language itself has tremendous spiritual power. If one does not know Hebrew, it is permissible to recite the prayer in English or any other language. The words have power in any language, but not as much as they have in the original. In order to use the Amidah as a meditation, on the other hand, one should be able to recite it in the original and know its meaning.

The Amidah was authored just before the close of the prophetic period two and a half thousand years ago, during the early years of the Second Temple in Jerusalem. Ezra had returned from Babylonia to the Holy Land and was rallying the people to reestablish Judaism as a viable way of life. Jerusalem and the Holy Land had been reduced to ashes by the Babylonians under Nebuchadnezzar, and it was out of these ashes that Ezra and his followers built Judaism anew.

Toward this end, Ezra gathered together one hundred and twenty of the greatest sages of his time. This group, which also included the last of the biblical prophets, was known as the Great Assembly (*keneseth ha-gedolah*). The Great Assembly enacted a number of important rules in order to preserve Torah observance among Jews scattered all over the world. One of the major accomplishments of the Great Assembly was to canonize the text of the Bible.

It was the Great Assembly that first authored the Amidah. The prayer is therefore one of the most ancient in existence today. Among its authors were Haggai, Zechariah, and Malachi, who also composed books of the Bible. The same spiritual energy that went into writing the Bible also went into writing the Amidah. It was designated as a universal prayer and meditation for all Jews from that time on.

The power of the Amidah comes from the words themselves. The prayer was carefully composed by highly advanced spiritual individuals so as to enable a maximum relationship with God. As we shall see, in the first paragraph, a person is drawn closer and closer to God, until he feels the presence of God all around him, penetrating his very being.

Since the Amidah was composed as a meditation prayer, it is necessary to repeat it as often as possible. It is for this reason that it was required that the same prayer be said three times every day.

As discussed earlier, one of the reasons a mantra works is that when the words are said over and over, the mind develops a special resonance with them. The words can then be said automatically, without special effort or concentration. Since the mind is not concerned with *saying* the words, it can allow itself to be filled with their meaning.

The same is true of a prayer that is said every day. Eventually, one not only memorizes the words, but learns to say them automatically. After one has recited the Amidah three times daily for a few years, one can literally say the prayer without thinking. While this is a danger, it is also a great advantage. The danger is that the mind will drift away from the words and the prayer will become meaningless. Indeed, many people who worship every day find it very difficult to keep their mind on what they are saying. If the Amidah is treated simply as prayer, this is a problem. However, if it is treated as a mantra, then the automatic nature of the recital is a great boon. The words themselves become like a mantra, quieting the mind and removing from it all extraneous thought.

Of course, this does not mean that one should not think about the words of the Amidah, but the way one thinks of the words becomes very different. Instead of thinking of them in an intellectual sense, one allows the words to resonate through the mind. It feels as if the words were conveying their message in a nonverbal manner.

Thus, when one says in the first blessing that God is "great," one has an overpowering experience of God's greatness. Similarly, when one says that He is "mighty," one experiences His infinite strength. Like many experiences in the meditative state, however, these feelings are difficult to describe.

The Amidah is a single unit that should be said in its entirety without interruption. As a practical matter, however, the first paragraph is the most important part of the Amidah, and it is this section that sets the tone for the rest of the prayer.

For a person who has worshiped every day, making the transition to using the Amidah as a meditation may involve a change in orientation. Nevertheless, one who knows the words well and has learned the methods of meditation in general can make the transition. One may have recited the Amidah for years, even from early childhood; the only thing necessary to learn is to say it effectively.

However, a person who is not familiar with the Amidah will have to go through a preparatory period in order to memorize the words and become familiar with them. This period should take a minimum of thirty days. It may be difficult for the neophyte to learn the entire Amidah that perfectly in this short time. Nevertheless, the first paragraph consists of only forty-two words and therefore can be readily learned. This paragraph itself can be the meditation, while the rest of the Amidah is then read as a prayer.

If at all possible, learn this first blessing in the original Hebrew. If you can read Hebrew but do not understand the words, learn at least the translation of these forty-two words. If you cannot read Hebrew, try to get someone to transliterate them and learn to recite them in Hebrew. The spiritual benefits that can be gained from this method are so great that it would be worthwhile to learn Hebrew for no other reason than to be able to say the Amidah in its original language.

During the preparatory period, memorize the first paragraph. This is important because this paragraph should be said with the eyes closed. Some authorities say that the entire Amidah should be recited by heart. These authorities state that this was the reason why no prayer books were used during the Talmudic period. Since some people could not recite the Amidah by heart, it was ordained that a reader would repeat the prayer aloud for those who could not say it by themselves.

Once you have memorized the first blessing, recite it by heart as part of the three prescribed services for at least thirty days. After this preparatory period, you should be familiar enough with the paragraph to use it as a meditative device.

To use the Amidah as a meditation, one must be familiar with its basic rules. Indeed, a number of these rules make sense only if one looks at the Amidah as a meditation.

The first rule is that the Amidah must be said at the proper time. The morning *shacharith* Amidah can be said from dawn until the end of the first quarter of the day (approximately 10:00 A.M.) or, in an emergency, until noon. The afternoon *minchah* Amidah can be said from shortly after noon until sunset. The evening *maariv* Amidah can be said from nightfall until just before dawn.

Before any worship service, one must wash the hands. This is reminiscent of the *kohen* priests, who would wash their hands before performing the Divine Service in the Jerusalem Temple. Washing the hands is more than mere cleansing; it is a ritual purification that must be done in a prescribed manner. The washing is accomplished by pouring water from a cup or glass, first over the right hand and then over the left hand, washing the hands in this manner three times alternately.

One may not recite the Amidah unless one is properly dressed. In particular, men should cover their heads with a hat or a *yarmulke*. It also should not be said in the presence of other people who are not decently dressed, or where an unpleasant odor is present. Preferably it should not be said in a situation where there is anything that will disturb one's concentration.

By definition, the Amidah is said while standing. The feet should be together, which, as the Talmud states, is the stance of the angels. The head can be slightly bowed and the hands be placed over the heart.

Whenever possible, one should face Jerusalem when reciting the Amidah. If one is in Jerusalem, one should face the site of the Temple. The physical location of the Temple is a source of spiritual energy, and facing in this direction helps draw this energy from the site of the Holy of Holies. According to ancient tradition, this was the place that Jacob called "the gate of heaven" (Gen. 28:17), and as such, it is the primary source of spiritual energy.

When one says the word "blessed" (*barukh*) at the beginning and end of the first paragraph, one should bend the knees. When one says the next word, "are you" (*attah*), one should bow down from the waist. This bowing is repeated again at the beginning and end of the Modim, which is the next-to-last section of the Amidah.

Bowing is integral to getting oneself into the meditative state. According to the Talmud, one bows down fairly quickly but then comes up very slowly, "like a snake." The commentaries explain that this means raising first the head and then the rest of the body. When one comes up in this manner, it slows the body's tempo and puts the mind in a quieter framework. It thus has the effect of quieting the mind and making it more receptive for meditation.

With the exception of bowing, it is preferable to remain absolutely motionless during the Amidah. Some people have the habit of shaking and swaying during this prayer, but the codes of Jewish law regard this more as a nervous habit than as a means of improving one's concentration. Both the Kabbalists and many major codifiers state explicitly that all motion should be avoided in the Amidah.

If you find it impossible to remain absolutely still, you may sway very lightly, but excessive shaking or swaying tends to impair concentration in a meditative sense.

It is also important to close the eyes in the Amidah, especially during the first blessing, in order to get yourself into a meditative state. If you do not know the rest of the Amidah by heart, it can be said from a prayerbook.

The words of the Amidah should be said quietly, either in a very soft voice or in a quiet whisper. The voice should be directed inward rather than outward.

These methods will make the Amidah a more effective instrument of worship. If the Amidah is also to be a meditation, there is one more important condition, and this has to do with the pace at which the words are said. The Talmud relates that the "original saints" (*chasidim rishonim*) used to take one hour to recite the Amidah. From the context, as well as from a number of Kabbalistic sources, it is obvious that these original saints used the Amidah as a meditation. This teaching provides an important clue to the pace at which the Amidah is to be said if it is to be used as a meditative device. A simple count shows that the entire Amidah contains approximately 500 words. The original saints took an hour to say it, or some 3,600 seconds. Therefore, they said this prayer at a pace of approximately one word every seven seconds.

To say the entire Amidah at this pace is a highly advanced form of meditation. However, this pace is not difficult to maintain for the first paragraph, which is the most important. Since the first blessing contains forty-two words, to say it at the rate of a word every seven seconds would take just under five minutes. This is a reasonable time, yet long enough to put one into a deep meditative state.

This pace has the effect of quieting the mind in a most profound manner. It is a meditative state that appears subjectively to be very different than that obtained through ordinary mantra meditation or contemplation because the words one is saying define the meditation at every point.

There are two basic ways in which you can pace the recitation of the words. You can draw out each word as long as possible and then pause briefly to let the meaning sink in. Alternatively, you can recite the word and then wait for seven seconds before saying the next word. Each method is effective in its own way, and either can be used, depending on your preference.

While reciting a word, and for the period afterward, do not think of anything other than the simple meaning of the word. (The significance of the words of the first paragraph of the Amidah will be discussed in the next chapter.) Allow the words to penetrate your inner being, opening yourself to feel and see the meaning of each word. During the pause between words, the mind is hushed in anticipation of the next word and then cleared of all other thought.

Once you have said the first blessing in this manner, the rest of the Amidah flows easily. It is then a simple matter to recite the entire Amidah with a feeling of closeness to God and without any extraneous thoughts.

Some people find it beneficial to combine the Amidah with a visualization technique. Some sources indicate that while reciting the first paragraph, one should attempt to visualize pure white light. Other sources state that one should visualize the letters of the Tetragrammaton. Still another source teaches that it is beneficial to visualize nothingness while saying this paragraph. The person who is familiar with these techniques may find them beneficial in enhancing the meditative experience of the Amidah. Another alternative is to concentrate on the spontaneous images that arise in the mind's eye.

Eventually, however, one learns that the most powerful technique of all is to use the words of the Amidah and nothing else. When the words will the mind, one becomes oblivious to all other thought. The words draw the person to God, and the mind becomes completely filled with the Divine. In this manner, the Amidah can bring a person to some of the most profound spiritual experiences possible. Since it was composed for this purpose, this is by no means surprising.

12 · Relating to God

As we discussed in the previous chapter, the first paragraph of the Amidah is the most important element of the service for use as a meditation. Moreover, this blessing defines the I–Thou relationship between the worshiper and God. Let us explore this paragraph word by word.

The first blessing of the Amidah is:

> Blessed are You, Adonoy,
>> our God and God of our fathers,
> God of Abraham, God of Isaac, and God of Jacob,
> Great, mighty, and awesome God,
>> Highest God,
> Doer of good, kind deeds,
>> Master of all,
> Who remembers the love of the Patriarchs
>> and brings a redeemer to their children's children
>>> for His name's sake,
>>>> with love.
> King, Helper, Rescuer, and Shield.
> Blessed are You, Adonoy, Shield of Abraham.

The first word of the Amidah is "blessed," *barukh* in Hebrew. It is difficult to understand what the term "blessed" means when applied to God. A person can be blessed to have life, health, prosperity, children, and other benefits. But what does it mean when we say that God is blessed?

If we look at blessings in the Bible, we always find that God is giving the recipient of the blessing some good or benefit. For example, Isaac says to Jacob, "May God give you from the dew of heaven and from the fat of the earth . . ." (Gen. 27:28). The main point of this and other blessings in the Bible is that God will be granting the recipient a special providence and that He will have a special relationship and closeness to the one receiving the blessing.

A blessing is therefore an expression of God's immanence. When we say that God is "blessed," we are saying that His immanent presence is the source of all blessing. This implies that God is close—very close—to us. Many Jewish sources indicate that the word "blessed" specifically denotes God's immanence in the world.

When we recite the word "blessed" (*barukh*) in the Amidah, we should be aware that God is very close, permeating the very air around us. We should feel God in our bones, in our flesh, in our minds, in the deepest recesses of our souls. We should also be aware that God makes Himself available in order to enhance our closeness to Him.

The next word is "You," *attah* in Hebrew. This word refers to the I–Thou relationship that we have with God. Simply saying "You" to God makes us aware that we are speaking directly to Him. When we say this word, we should be aware of the Divine directly in front of us and feel all the love, strength, and awe that exist when we confront the Divine.

Then comes God's name, which in Hebrew is pronounced *Adonoy*. This name is actually written as the Tetragrammaton, YHVH, but since this most holy name may not be pronounced, the name Adonoy, which means "my Lord," is substituted. This substitution teaches us some very important lessons about the Divine.

The meaning of the Tetragrammaton on one level has been

discussed in chapter 7. However, there is another way of understanding this name on an even deeper level.

The codes note that the Tetragrammaton, YHVH, appears to be related to the past, present, and future of the Hebrew verb "to be"; in Hebrew, "was" is *hayah*, "is" is *hoveh*, and "will be" is *yihyeh*. Therefore, the codes state, when one sees the Tetragrammaton, one should have in mind that God "was, is, and will be"—all at once. This indicates that God is utterly transcendental, higher even than the realm of time. God exists in a realm where time does not exist.

This also implies that God is totally different from anything else in creation. We cannot even begin to imagine a being existing outside of space, for whom the very concept of space does not apply. It is even more difficult to imagine a being who exists outside of time, so much so that past, present, and future are all the same to Him. Our very thought processes are dependent on time and can function only within the framework of time. Yet none of this applies to God.

Of course, even to use the word "being" with relation to God is a misnomer and anthropomorphism. The only reason that we think of God as a "being" is so that we can speak to Him, and "being" is the only category into which we can fit that to which we can speak. Of course, the fact that "being" is the closest category into which we can place God does not mean that He is a being. As we have discussed earlier, there is no category into which we can place God.

There are two major supercategories in our minds into which all things can be placed: that of things and that of relationships or states. If we could place God in the category of things, then we would speak of Him as a being. However, if we placed Him in the category of relationships, we would speak of Him as a principle. Thus, when we say that "God is the creator of the universe," we are speaking of Him as a being. On the other hand, when we say, "God is the creative force in the universe," we are speaking of Him as a principle.

The first time I used this concept in a class, one of my students asked a simple but very tricky question: "If God exists outside of space, how can we say that God is everywhere?" After a few moments of thought, the idea struck me. I asked the class, "Does the equation $1 + 1 = 2$ exist in space?"

The class's response was that this equation obviously does not exist in space. The equation $1 + 1 = 2$ is not a thing that can exist in space, but rather a mathematical relationship. It is a mathematical *principle,* and as such, it exists in the world of ideas, and not in space.

Then I asked another question: "Is there any place where $1 + 1 = 2$ does not exist?"

The obvious answer was no. Wherever one would go in the entire universe—and beyond—one would find that $1 + 1 = 2$. This simple equation is a good example of something that does not exist in space and yet, at the same time, exists everywhere. This is true of every universal principle. By nature, an abstract principle is not spatial and therefore exists outside of space. Yet, if we are speaking of a universal principle, such as any of the principles of mathematics, there is no place where it does not exist.

For many purposes, it would be useful to think of God as a principle rather than a being. For one thing, it would make it readily understandable how He exists outside of space and time, and yet fills all space and time. For another, an idea such as this breaks down the anthropomorphic ideas that people have about God.

One may be tempted to say, "God is a principle." However, as I discussed earlier, the sentence "God is . . ." is a statement that cannot be completed. God is the creator of all categories and therefore cannot fit into any of them. Both "principle" and "being" are approximations that we use because the mind has no category into which it can place God. It may be that a third, intermediate category might be a better approximation, but the mind has no example of it, and therefore, such a category cannot be imagined. Nevertheless, through meditation, one can gain a glimmer of the nature of this third category.

The Tetragrammaton appears to relate to God as a principle

rather than as a being. It denotes God's existence in the past, the present, and the future simultaneously, just like that of any other principle. Earlier, I discussed how the Tetragrammaton denotes the four steps in the process through which God gives existence to His creation (see chapter 8). In this respect, we are also seeing the Tetragrammaton as describing God as the creative principle.

Nevertheless, it is not easy to relate to a principle, which appears totally impersonal, and indeed is. In prayer and worship, it is much easier to relate to God as a being. Therefore, we do not pronounce the Tetragrammaton, but instead substitute *Adonoy*, "my Lord." This indicates that God is Lord and Master of all creation. In seeing God as Lord and Master, we are viewing Him as a being rather than as a principle. Mastery and dominance are anthropomorphic concepts that are most fitting to a sentient being.

As we reach the name of God that is written as the Tetragrammaton and pronounced *Adonoy*, we become aware that we are addressing a Being-Principle. We see God as the Principle that gives existence to all things. Yet, at the same time, we see God as a Being, and furthermore, as a Being to whom we can relate. When we speak to God, it is as if we are communing with existence itself, but at the same time speaking to it as if it were a person. At the same time, we realize that God is more than existence, actually the principle that allows existence to be.

When we pronounce God's name, *Adonoy*, we are aware that we are addressing the Infinite Being who is the absolute Other. The very next word, however, is *Elohenu*, which is translated as "our God." This shows the extent to which God allows us to relate to Him and draw close. As far above us as He is, He allows us to address Him as "our God"—as if, in a sense, He belonged to us. This is perhaps the greatest gift and miracle of all—that God allows us to call Him "ours."

The full expression in which we address God as ours is "our God and God of our fathers" (*Elohenu ve-Elohey avotenu*). The Baal Shem Tov explains this expression in the following manner:

There are two ways in which we can know God. First, we know about God because we have heard about Him from others. We have inherited a tradition about God from our fathers, from our ancestors, and from all the great people of the past.

This, however, is not enough. No matter how much a person may have heard about God, he must also have his own personal experience of God. Unless a person has experienced God for himself, he will never have any true idea of what God is. In a way, it is like love. If you have ever been in love, then you know what I mean when I speak about love. But if you have never been in love, the word is totally abstract. You may imagine that love is something very nice, but you have no experience of it. Even if you read what poets sing about love, you can understand it only on the most abstract level. However, if you have ever been in love, the word will have very powerful connotations for you.

The same is true of God. If you have experienced closeness to God even once in your life, then when I speak about God, you know exactly what I mean, and the concept has a very strong spiritual connotation. But if you have never had this experience, then God is something very abstract and can be described only on an intellectual level. We can speak about God, argue about Him, and even debate His existence. However, if you have ever experienced God, then there is nothing to talk about. As soon as I mention the word "God," you know exactly what I am speaking about, since God is as much part of your experience as He is of mine. One who has never been in love might argue that love does not exist. The same is true of one who has never experienced God. But for one who has had the experience, there is no question.

When one experiences God, however, there is always the danger that it is a false experience. That is, you may think that you are experiencing God, but you may actually be experiencing something very different.

It is for this reason that we say "and God of our fathers." The experience of God is not something that we are inventing, something that has no relation to our past. Rather, it is part of a tradition that goes back to our earliest ancestors. We affirm that we are not going off in our quest for God on our own, but doing so as part of an unbroken chain of tradition.

We then say, "God of Abraham, God of Isaac, and God of Jacob." We mention the Patriarchs because we see them as having attained the ultimate experience of God. For them the experience of God was so strong that they were willing to challenge their environment and change their lives because of it, becoming the spiritual trailblazers for millions that followed them. At this opening point in the Amidah, we attempt to direct our consciousness to the level of closeness to God that the Patriarchs had experienced.

It is taught that Abraham's primary experience of God was that of His greatness, whereas Isaac experienced God's strength and Jacob experienced His awesomeness. Thus, the peak experiences of the Patriarchs correspond to the next three expressions in the Amidah, "the great, mighty, and awesome God."

When one says that God is "great" (*ha-gadol*) in the Amidah, one should concentrate on greatness and immensity. Try to imagine how great God is. Think of the size of the largest thing you can imagine. Then go further and try to imagine the size of the planet Earth. Continue, and imagine the size of the sun, the solar system, the galaxy, and then the entire universe. Then realize how tiny this all is in comparison with the greatness of God. Compared with Him, the entire universe is less than a mote of dust.

This, of course, is contemplation on an intellectual level, and during the Amidah is not the time for such intellectualizing. When we say the expression "the great," we have to take the concept of greatness beyond the intellectual level. The mind expands with the concept of greatness and becomes aware of greatness and bigness in its purest and most abstract form. The concept of greatness reverberates through one's entire being, and one can then catch a glimpse of what it means in relation to God.

In Kabbalah, God's greatness is closely associated with His love (*chesed*). When we imagine an Infinite Being ready to listen to the voice of an infinitesimal creature, we realize that there can be no greater love. Thus, in the greatness, there is also love. This is another reason that Abraham is associated with God's attribute of greatness and love. It is taught that Abraham directed his life to emulate God's love. Abraham was an important personage in his time, with sufficient status to rub shoulders with kings and monarchs. Nevertheless, he would literally run to greet and serve even the lowliest of wayfarers (see Gen. 18:3,4).

The next word is "the mighty" (*ha-gibbor*). When one says this word, one should think of God's strength. Earlier, I mentioned how one can look at one's own hand and see the strength in it. When one says the word "the mighty," one should likewise concentrate on strength in its pure form. When one thinks about strength in terms of God, it expands until it overwhelms the mind. One then begins to have an inkling of strength as it applies to God.

Finally, we say, "and the awesome" (*ve-ha-norah*). This emulates the experience of Jacob at Bethel after he saw the vision of God and the ladder, when he said, "How awesome is this place!" (Gen. 28:17). When one is aware of God's greatness and strength, one is overcome with a feeling of awe. Rather than being a frightening experience, it is a sweet and beautiful awe, the awe that comes from standing in the presence of the Infinite.

The next phrase is "highest God" (*El Elyon*). This expression is designated to make us realize that when we say that God is "great, mighty, and awesome," these adjectives are not meant to limit Him in any way, but merely name the emotions and experiences that we have when we try to draw close to God. When one attempts to approach God, as we do in the Amidah, one first has a sensation of infinite greatness, then a feeling of infinite strength, and finally a feeling of overwhelming awe.

It is important to realize that God is above all these. The mind must therefore soar above greatness, above strength, above awe, and realize that God transcends any thought that we can possibly have. God is beyond the sky, beyond the stars, beyond the heavens, and even beyond the spiritual realm.

This last concept is important to reiterate. Often people speak of God as a Spirit or as being spiritual. However, God is above the spiritual just as He is above the physical. Just as He is the creator of the concept of the physical, He is also the creator of the concept of the spiritual. As creator of the spiritual, He cannot be encompassed by it. Therefore, as high as our concept of God may be, it cannot even begin to come close to His true essence. The Amidah puts this very succinctly when it refers to Him as "highest God."

Immediately after saying that God is the ineffable "highest God," we say that He is the "Doer of good, kind deeds." Although God is higher than any thought can conceive, He still does things that we can perceive as being kind and good. Therefore, when we say these words, we are aware of God's infinite goodness and kindness.

This is very closely related to a Talmudic teaching: "Wherever you find mention of God's greatness, you also find mention of His humility." What the Talmud is saying is that an Infinite Being is not limited by any human conception of greatness or smallness. God is so great that to Him a galaxy is no more significant than a bacterium. At the same time, He is great enough that a single human being can be as significant to Him as an entire universe.

After this, we speak of God as *koney ha-kol*, which has been translated as "Master of all," but which would be more literally translated as "Owner of all." Just as an owner can do as he pleases with his property, so God can do as He wills with all things. All creation is God's property, and He can do with it as He wills. Moreover, an owner takes possession of his property and associates it with his person. In a certain sense, anything a person owns is an extension of the self. In a similar manner, God associates Himself with His creation, and His essence permeates all existence.

The Amidah then links the past to the future, saying that God "remembers the love of the Patriarchs and brings a redeemer to their children's children. . . ." God thus shares our memory of the past, especially with regard to the Patriarchs, who were the first ones to bring God consciousness to the world. Just as we look to the Patriarchs for a paradigm of the God experience, God looks at their love for Him as a paradigm, and as a reason to remain close to their descendants no matter what happens.

We also see God as our hope in the future—no small thing in

this age over which hangs a Damocles' sword of nuclear destruction. We believe that God will bring a redeemer, who will make the world a safe and sane place to live. We have faith that there will come a time when all humanity will be brought back to the God consciousness that the Patriarchs enjoyed and that this will be a time of universal peace and good for all humankind. This is our ultimate hope in the future.

We conclude by saying that God remembers the Patriarchs and will bring a redeemer "for His name's sake." As we discussed earlier, God's name is much more than an arbitrary collection of sounds. Rather, it is a word that speaks of His essence and His relationship with creation. The name is an important focus of our God consciousness, as I have discussed in previous chapters.

God's name also figures both in the lives of the Patriarchs and in our hope in the future. The experience of the Patriarchs was always closely linked to God's name. The Torah tells that Abraham began his career by "calling in the name of God" (Gen. 12:8). The Patriarchs were thus the ones who initiated God consciousness to the world through His name. Not only did they link themselves to the Infinite, but they also identified It with a name.

The process begun by the Patriarchs will be completed by the promised redeemer, who will bring God's name to all humanity. One of the important prophecies regarding the messianic future is that "On that day, God will be One and His Name One" (Zech. 14:9). Not only will the entire world worship God, but everyone will call Him by the same name. This will indicate that the whole world will have the same God consciousness as the heirs of the Patriarchs. The Amidah expresses this by stating that the entire process will be "for His name's sake."

The initial portion ends with the expression "with love" (*be-ahavah*). It is love that bridges the gap between the past and future—even as love bridges the gap between man and woman. In a sense, the past and future can be looked upon as a male and a female. Just as the male impregnates the female, the past impregnates the future. The redemption in the future will come from the memory of the Patriarchs in the past. It is God's love spanning the chasm of time.

Moreover, God causes the processes of history to unfold, the goal being the perfection of humanity and society. This entire process is governed by love. We make ourselves aware of God's love at this point in the Amidah, and are totally saturated by it.

The first paragraph in the Amidah concludes with four words that are designated to bring God closer to the worshiper. These four words are "King, Helper, Rescuer, and Shield." Whereas in the first part of this paragraph we relate to God in a general manner, here we develop our personal relationship with Him.

These four words are the key to the entire Amidah. If one says them correctly, one is left in a perfect spiritual space for the rest of the service. Even if one has said the first parts of this paragraph without proper concentration, if these four words are said properly, they will bring the worshiper to such a closeness to God that the rest of the Amidah will be perfect. If one cannot say the entire first paragraph at the rate of seven seconds per word, as mentioned earlier, one should at least do so for these four words.

Let us look at these four words in detail.

The first word is "King" (*Melekh*). We begin by looking at God as our king and at our relationship to Him as that of a subject to a king. A king is far away, in his capital city, in his palace. If you want something from the king, you must send him a formal request, and it goes through his staff, his ministers, his secretary. Then, if you are lucky, after a few months you may get a reply. Therefore, when we address God as King, we see Him as majestic but distant. Help is available from him, but not closely available.

In the next word, we address God as "Helper" (*Ozer*). Now we see him as much closer than a king. A "helper" is someone whom we can readily approach. He is a friend whom we know we can always call on and who always will make himself available. Therefore, when we call God "Helper," we realize that we can call on Him at any time and He will be there for us. This is a relationship much closer than that to a king. In saying this word, we are beginning the process through which we draw closer to God.

Third, we address God as "Rescuer" (*Moshia*). Again, a rescuer is much closer than a helper. A rescuer is someone who is available to save you when you are drowning in a river; he is right there to jump in and pull you out. A helper may have the best intentions in the world, but if he is not close to you at all times, he cannot save you when you are in danger. Therefore, when we speak to God as our "Rescuer," we see Him as being available whenever we need Him, ready to rescue us in an instant. We recognize that God is always close enough to help us, even when we are in imminent danger. Thus, the relationship of Rescuer is much closer than that of Helper. This word brings us yet a step closer to God.

Finally, we speak to God as our "Shield" (*Magen*). A shield is even closer than a rescuer. A shield can help even when an arrow is flying at me and there is nothing else that can stop it. When the arrow is flying, there is no time for even the rescuer to intercept it. The shield must be there in place—right in front of me. Thus, when I address God as my "Shield," I can feel Him right in front of me. God is all around me, surrounding me like a suit of divine armor. I am totally aware of God's protective power, surrounding me on all sides. I feel that I am being protected by God, so that nothing in the world can harm me.

Thus, in the four words "King, Helper, Rescuer, and Shield," we become more and more aware of God's closeness. First we see Him as a benevolent but distant king, then as a willing helper, then as an nearby rescuer, and finally, as an immanent shield. In these four words, we make the transition from viewing God as a remote transcendental force to seeing Him as a protector who is closer than the air around us.

The one person who reached the level where he could constantly see God as his shield was Abraham. God had told him, "Do not fear, Abram, I am a shield to you" (Gen. 15:1). From that time on, Abraham had a constant perception of God as his shield. He was always aware of God being very close to him, surrounding him and protecting him on a most immanent and direct level.

It is for this reason that the first paragraph ends with the blessing "Blessed are You, Adonoy, Shield of Abraham." It makes us aware that such a level of God consciousness exists and that it can even be woven into a way of life, as in the case of Abraham. Of all the levels of relationship to God, the level of shield is the closest. Here we see God close enough to us to stop even a flying bullet. This was the level attained by Abraham, and at this point in the Amidah, we aspire to it.

The word "blessed" (*barukh*) occurs twice in this first paragraph. The paragraph begins with the word "blessed," and then it is repeated in the ending, "Blessed are You, Adonoy, Shield of Abraham." It is significant that it was ordained that we bow at each of these points.

As discussed earlier, the word "blessed" indicates God's immanence and His power of blessing, which permeates all creation. We bow when we say "blessed" to indicate that we are aware of this immanence. We feel that God is directly in front of us, and we are bowing to this Presence.

By the time we reach the end of the paragraph, we have raised our consciousness of God's immanence considerably. At the beginning of the blessing, we were aware of God's immanence, but only in an abstract sense. At the end, our consciousness of God's immanence is such that it is as tangible and palpable as a shield. To indicate our new awareness, we bow a second time.

There are two other places at which we also bow in the Amidah. These are at the beginning and end of the blessing of thanksgiving (Modim), which is the second-from-the-last section of the Amidah. To understand the reason for this, we must first understand the structure of the Amidah as a whole.

It is taught that the essential structure of any prayer should contain three elements—adoration, petition, and thanksgiving, in that order. This structure is maintained in the Amidah. The first three paragraphs consist of adoration, wherein we establish a degree of God consciousness in the mind. The first paragraph is the key to this process, as we have seen.

The second general part of the Amidah is that of petition, wherein we ask God for certain things. This part consists of the next fourteen blessings of the Amidah. It is significant to note that in Hebrew, the number fourteen is written out as *yod daleth*

(**T'**), which also spells *yad*, the Hebrew word for "hand." As it were, we are asking that our petitions be answered through God's hand.

What we are doing essentially in the petition stage is using the spiritual energy developed in the first three blessings to bring about the things we want, both as individuals and as a nation. First we ask for our own personal needs, petitioning God for wisdom, closeness, atonement, healing, and blessing. Then we ask for the things that will affect the Israelite people as a whole. The latter part of the petition stage thus deals primarily with redemption.

According to this pattern, the Amidah should end with thanksgiving. In thanking God, we show awareness of the closeness and spiritual energy that He allows us to experience, and thus integrate it into our being. We would therefore expect the Amidah to end with the blessing of thanksgiving, or Modim, as it is called. Actually, however, this blessing is the second from the last.

There is an important reason for this, and that is so that the Amidah can end with a petition and blessing for peace. Once one has drawn down spiritual energy, one can find internal peace. This internal peace can be projected to enhance national and universal peace as well. When a person can fully thank God, in a mystical as well as a mundane sense, he is at perfect peace. In thanking God, we also draw in the energy that is developed in the service. The bowing acknowledges the power of God that we have drawn into our essence. Since this is the purpose of the blessing of thanksgiving, we bow once at its beginning and again at its end.

Bowing in the Amidah also has another important connotation. The Talmud states that one of the reasons why the Amidah has eighteen blessings is that they parallel the eighteen vertebrae of the spine and neck. The nineteenth blessing, which was added later, parallels the coccyx, the small bone at the base of the spine. This brings to mind the concept of *kundalini* energy that is discussed in Eastern teachings. This is not to suggest that there is any relationship between the Jewish teaching and that of the East, but merely to point out that the spine is universally recognized as an important conduit of energy. Moreover, whereas in *kundalini* meditation one strives to elevate energy from the base of the spine to the head, in the Amidah one brings energy from the mind to the rest of the body.

The Talmud also teaches that if one does not bow in the blessing of thanksgiving, one's spine turns into a snake. Obviously this is to be taken not in a physical sense, but in a spiritual meaning. One reason the Talmud gives for the number of blessings corresponding to the number of vertebrae is that one must bow low enough for each vertebra to be separated from the one next to it. The Talmud also teaches that when one bows, one should do so like a rod, but when one rises, one should do so like a serpent, raising the head first and then the body.

The *kundalini* energy is also seen as taking the form of a serpent. In Jewish tradition, however, the serpent is seen as the enemy of mankind. The serpent is the tempter, who tries to use sexual energy to draw humans away from God. The Talmud therefore teaches that if one does not bow during the Amidah, then one's spine turns into a snake. In contrast, the posture in *kundalini* meditation requires that the spine be kept perfectly straight and erect. If a person worships in this manner, without bowing, then his spine will become infused with the *kundalini* energy, which is the serpent.

Bowing may be a way of overcoming this energy of the serpent. The concept of *kundalini* is to bring energy up from the sexual area to the rest of the body. Bowing has the opposite connotation, namely that of bringing energy down from the head to the body. Therefore, when we bow, we lower the head toward the body. Only after we have bowed, and infused the body with spiritual energy, can we rise and lift energy from the spine to the head, "rising like a snake."

In this manner, the Amidah is designed to bring spiritual energy through the spine to the entire body. This is also a reason why this prayer is said with the feet together. As I have said, this is the stance in which angels are visualized. During the Amidah, one strives to bring oneself into an angelic mode, wherein the spiritual becomes dominant over the physical.

13 · Unification

The most ancient and most important Jewish prayer is the Shema. This prayer consists of the words:

Shema Yisrael, Adonoy Elohenu, Adonoy Echad.
Listen, Israel, Adonoy, our God, Adonoy is One.

The words themselves are taken from the Torah (Deut. 6:4). In many ways this sentence can be looked upon as the most important verse in the Torah. First, the Torah designates that it be recited twice every day, in the morning and in the evening. It is also the key element in the parchment in the *tefillin* that are worn during daily worship, as well as in the *mezuzah* that is affixed to the doorpost.

The Shema is more than just a prayer. It is the basic declaration of faith for the Jew. It is one of the first things a Jew learns as a child, and the last words one is to say before dying. All through life, one is to say this sentence twice a day, without fail.

It would seem that the Shema would be perfect to use as a mantra. The Talmud, however, discourages this as a practice and says that one who repeats the Shema should be silenced. The concept of the Shema is that of unity, and therefore it is meant to be said only once at a time.

The Talmud notes that the Shema has the unique ability to

dispel the forces of evil. The Shema is said in bed, just before one goes to sleep at night. According to the Talmud, night is the time when the forces of evil are strongest, and the Shema has the power to protect us against them.

The reason for this should be obvious: evil has power only when it is seen as disconnected from God. If one thinks that there can be a force of evil apart from God, then one can be harmed by it. However, if a person recognizes that even evil is a creation of God, then it no longer has any power over him. God Himself said through His prophet, "I form light and create darkness, I make peace and create evil; I am God, I do all these things" (Isa. 45:7).

The Zohar explains the existence of evil with a parable. A king once wanted to test his son to see if he would be a worthy heir to the throne. He told his son to keep away from loose women and to remain virtuous. Then he hired a woman to entice his son, instructing her to use all her wiles with him. The Zohar then asks the rhetorical question: Is the woman not also a loyal servant of the king?

The purpose of evil is to tempt us and allow us to have free choice. Without the existence of evil, we would have no other choice but to do good and there would be no virtue in the good we do. But since God gave us free will and wants us to do good as a matter of our own free choice, evil plays a highly important role in His plan.

In the parable, as soon as the prince realizes that the woman is in the hire of his father, she is no longer a threat. The same is true of evil. Indeed, the Baal Shem Tov goes further in using this Zoharic teaching. He says, "Do not succumb to evil; emulate it." He explains that if evil is a loyal servant of the King, then you should be equally loyal. If evil does God's will, you should strive to do it equally well.

It is told that the great saint Rabbi Israel Meir ha-Kohen (1838–1933), better known as the Chafetz Chaim, related that he once woke up on a cold winter morning to say his prayers. The Evil Urge said to him, "How can you get up so early? You are already an old man, and it's so cold outside." The Chafetz Chaim replied to the Evil Urge, "You're a lot older than me, and you're up already." This also illustrates the concept of emulating evil rather than succumbing to it.

In any case, the Shema declares that God is One. If God is One, then His purpose must also be One. Since God's purpose in creation was to do good, then the only reason that evil exists is to enhance the world's ultimate good. If a person has a deep realization of this, then the forces of evil have no power over him.

A paradigm of this attitude can be found in the great Rabbi Akiva (c. 50–135 C.E.). Rabbi Akiva's watchword always was, "All that the Merciful One does is for the good." Rabbi Akiva faced his greatest test during the Hadrianic persecutions of the Jews around 135 C.E. The Romans had decreed that no one could teach Torah, under penalty of death, but Rabbi Akiva ignored them and carried on his vocation as Torah teacher. He was captured and sentenced to be killed by having his flesh torn away by curry combs, a most excruciating torture. Still, while he was being tortured to death in this manner, he told his students that he was happy, since he had been given the opportunity to suffer and die as an expression of his love for God. Death and torture held no terror for him, since he had a love that was more powerful than death.

Significantly, Rabbi Akiva's last words were the Shema. Even in the midst of his most terrible suffering, he was able to see God's unity and oneness, and therefore he could see God even in his suffering. Rabbi Akiva had been a student of Nachum Ish Gamzu for twenty-two years. Nachum was called Gamzu because, no matter what happened to him, he would say, "This too [*gam zu*] is for the good." Like his student, Nachum suffered terribly during his lifetime, but no matter what happened to him, he was able to see it as good.

The Shema is an integral part of the morning *shacharith* and evening *maariv* service. Together with a number of important prayers that surround it, it is said immediately before the Amidah. However, the Shema can also be said alone, as an important meditation in its own right.

From the wording itself, it is obvious that the Shema was

meant to be a meditation. If the only significance of the Shema were to declare that God is One, then the opening words, "Listen, Israel," would be redundant. But the Shema itself is telling us to *listen*—to listen and hear the message with every fiber of our being. It is telling us to open our perceptions completely, so as to experience God's unity.

It is also significant that the name Israel is used in the beginning of the declaration. This name was given to Jacob after he wrestled with the angel on his way home to Canaan. According to the Torah, the name Israel means "he who contends with the Divine" (Gen. 32:29).

In the Midrash and the Zohar, there is discussion about whether the angel with which Jacob wrestled was a good angel or an evil one. But the main point is that when a person contends with the spiritual, he is opening himself up to both good and evil, which means wrestling with the forces of good as well as those of evil.

A number of commentaries see Jacob's experience as having taken place in a meditative state. Jacob did not physically wrestle with an angel, but he perceived a spiritual being while meditating. The name Israel that Jacob received would then pertain to his entering into a spiritual state and contending with his experiences there.

It is precisely when one is in a meditative state that one has contact with the spiritual on an intimate level. The Shema addresses itself to such a seeker and calls him by the name Israel. The Shema is addressing the "Israel" in each one of us. This "Israel" is the part of us that yearns to transcend the boundaries of the physical and seeks out the spiritual. The Shema tells this "Israel" to listen—to quiet down the mind completely and open it up to a universal message of God's unity. However, the only time a person can listen perfectly, without any interference, is in the meditative state.

The Shema then says, "Adonoy, our God" (*Adonoy Elohenu*). This is the same expression encountered earlier in the previous chapter, in our discussion of the Amidah. As mentioned there, we recognize that God is a totally different entity Who exists outside even the realms of space and time. When we say "Adonoy," we are speaking of that for which the mind does not even have a category. Yet, in the very next word, we call *Adonoy* "our God." We recognize that we can relate to God and experience His closeness to such an extent that we can call Him ours.

This is a very remarkable concept: we can think about the Infinite and still call It ours. The fact that God allows us to call Him "our God" is the greatest possible gift.

The Shema ends with "Adonoy is One" (*Adonoy Echad*). Here we are saying that no matter how many different ways we experience the Divine, they are all One and all have one source. We recognize that there is a basic Oneness in the universe and beyond, and in our search for the transcendental, it is precisely this Oneness that we are seeking. We see in God the most absolute Unity imaginable, the Oneness that unifies all creation.

The more we realize this, the more we begin to see that on an ultimate level there is no plurality. If there is no plurality, then we are also one with God. When saying the word "One" (*Echad*) in the Shema, one can realize this in a deep sense.

An objection might be raised here. If a person is one with God, how can he continue to exist? If he is one with God, then there is no room left for him to have an independent personality. How is it possible for a person to ever experience this oneness with God? The answer is that this situation is a paradox. To say that I exist and that God exists, and that I am one with God, is like saying $1 + 1 = 1$, which is, of course, logically impossible.

Nevertheless, we cannot say that logic is higher than God. Quite the contrary. Just as God created everything else, He also created logic. Logic is a tool of God's, but He is never bound by it. Therefore, if He wants one plus one to be one, it is no problem for Him. And if He wants a person to be one with Him, and still be able to experience it, it is also possible for Him.

This principle allows us to understand all theological paradoxes. To a large degree, in creating the world, God bound Himself by logic. Since He created man in "His image," man uses the same logic that went into creation and can therefore understand God's creation. However, when it suits God's purpose in creation to transcend logic, He can also do so, and this is what we perceive as paradox. Indeed, the concept of Divine will itself is a paradox. If God is the Creator of *all things*, then He must also be the Creator of the very concept of will. But how could God create will without this in itself being an act of will? In a sense, the creation of will is by its very nature paradoxical, like trying to pull yourself up by your own bootstraps.

The most powerful expression of will is love. This is also an integral part of the Shema. Every Hebrew letter has a numerical value corresponding to its position in the alphabet. The value of *echad* (אחד), the Hebrew word for "one," is thirteen (1 + 8 + 4). This, however, is the numerical value of *ahavah* (אהבה, 1 + 5 + 2 + 5), the Hebrew word for "love." Love is the power that breaks down barriers and unifies opposites. Two people who are deeply in love become one. The Torah says, "A man shall leave his father and mother, and attach himself to his wife, and they shall become *one* flesh" (Gen. 2:24). But the love and unity between God and man is greater than any possible between man and woman.

There are a number of prayers or "blessings" that surround the Shema when it is said as part of the morning service. The last words before the Shema itself are "Blessed are You, Adonoy, who chose His people Israel in love." Therefore, the word immediately before the Shema is the word "love," in the context of a blessing that speaks of the love that God has for His people.

Immediately after the Shema is the commandment "You shall love God your Lord with all your heart, with all your soul, and with all your might" (Deut. 6:5). This commandment speaks of the love that we must have for God. Therefore, the Shema is placed between two loves—God's love for us and our love for God. Both of these loves suggest the unity to be found in the Shema.

The Shema can be said as a prayer or a declaration of faith, and it is said as such by Jews all over the world. But if the words are said very slowly, and if a person prepares himself mentally, the Shema can be an extremely powerful meditation. Indeed, the Torah itself prescribes that the Shema be said twice daily, and it seems highly probable that this was originally prescribed as a short daily meditation for all Israel.

The technique consists in saying the words very slowly, in a manner very similar to that of using the Amidah for a meditation. In the Amidah, as noted in chapter 11, the prescribed rate was approximately one word every seven seconds. The Shema can be said even more slowly. You can dwell on each word for as long as fifteen or twenty seconds, or with experience, even longer. During the silences between words, let the meaning of each word penetrate your innermost being.

It is easier to use the Shema as a meditation than the Amidah, since the main portion of the Shema consists of only six words, which are easy to memorize. Before you can use these words as a meditation, you must know them well and by heart. You should be seated while saying the Shema and keep your eyes closed. Strive to be perfectly still, with no body motion whatsoever.

The Shema can be used as a meditation either as part of the regular services or alone. It is preferable to say it as part of the service, especially the morning service, which provides a proper setting and introduction to the Shema. In this service, the Shema is preceded by two prayers, or "blessings," as the Talmud calls them. The first blessing begins with a description of the astronomical world. The mind soars to the sun, the moon, the stars, and beyond, and contemplates the vast reaches of space, immense beyond comprehension. Yet, while one meditates on the vastness of the astronomical world, one sees it as all working to do God's will.

The mind then transcends the astronomical world and reaches up to the spiritual realm, to the world of the angels. We join the angels in their daily praise to God: "Holy, holy, holy, is the Lord of Hosts, the whole world is filled with His glory" (Isa. 6:3) and then, "Blessed be God's glory from His place" (Ezek. 3:12). One's mind reaches higher and higher, joining the highest angels in their quest for the Divine.

Then one enters the second blessing, which speaks of the "World of Love." Here we meditate on the love that God has shown us and how He drew us close to Him through the Torah and the commandments. We become aware of this love and meditate on it, drawing it into our innermost being. Then, we recite the Shema itself.

When the Shema is said as part of the morning service, one automatically goes through all these levels. However, even if one says the Shema alone as a meditation, one can go through all these levels as part of one's personal preparation. In either case, the Shema becomes not only a meditation, but a peak experience of love and closeness to God.

The words immediately following the Shema are usually translated in the imperative—"You *shall* love God, your Lord . . ."—implying that this is a commandment. However, the words can equally well be translated as "You *will* love God, your Lord," as a simple statement. The words imply that if we listen, and hear the message that God is ours and that He is One, then we will automatically love God. Love for God follows as a natural consequence to the experience of His essence and unity.

There is also another important element in the Shema as a meditation, and this concerns the actual spelling of the word. The first word, *shema* (שׁ מ ע), is spelled *shin* (שׁ) *mem* (מ) *ayin* (ע). In the *Sefer Yetzirah*, the *shin* and *mem* are described as two of the three "mother letters."

It is easy to understand why the *shin* and *mem* are important. The *shin* has the sound of *s* or *sh*, and hence, of all the letters in the alphabet, it has the sound closest to white noise. White noise is sound that contains every possible wavelength, and is usually heard as a hissing sound. On an oscilloscope, the *s* sound would appear as a totally chaotic jumble with no structure whatsoever.

The opposite of white noise is pure harmonic sound. This is a hum, like the sound of a tuning fork. On an oscilloscope, this would appear as a perfect wavy line, the epitome of order and regularity. This is the sound of the *mem*.

The *shin* thus represents chaos, while the *mem* represents harmony. The *Sefer Yetzirah* says that the *shin* represents fire, while the *mem* represents water. The *shin* denotes a hot, chaotic state of consciousness, while the *mem* denotes a cool, harmonic state. This is significant, since in many meditative traditions, the *m* sound is seen as one that leads to tranquillity and inner peace. The sound itself seems to be conducive to the harmony that one seeks in the meditative state. The *s* or *sh* sound, on the other hand, is more closely associated with our normal, everyday level of consciousness. It is also interesting to note that the "still small voice" (1 Kings 19:12) in which Elijah heard God is translated by the *Sefer Yetzirah* as a "fine humming sound." It appears that the *m* sound was closely associated with prophecy.

Many of the Hebrew words that tend to focus the mind on a single object are made up of these two mother letters. Thus, the Hebrew word for "name" is *shem* (**שֵׁם**), which is spelled *shin mem*. Similarly, the word for "there" is *sham* (**שָׁם**). Both of these words have the connotation of the transition from the chaos of the general to the harmony of the particular. A name separates a single object from the chaos of all objects, while "there" separates a place from the chaos of all places. Both words therefore denote the transition from the concept of the *shin* to that of the *mem*.

An exercise discussed by the commentaries on the *Sefer Yetzirah* has been found effective for getting into the meditative state quickly and simply. It consists of alternating the sounds of the *shin* and the *mem*. First pronounce one sound for the period of normal exhalation, then inhale and pronounce the other for the same period of time. The pattern is: "ssssss," inhale, "mmmmmm," inhale, "ssssss," inhale, "mmmmmm," inhale, and so on. The inhalation is silent and represents the third mother letter, the silent *alef* (**א**). This meditative method of alternating between the *s* and *m* sounds draws one deeper and deeper into the *m* sound. If one practices this exercise for a period of time, one can attain the ability to get into the meditative state merely by humming the *m* sound.

The fact that the first two letters of the Shema are *shin* and *mem* is highly significant. True listening involves a transition from normal "*shin*" consciousness to meditative "*mem*" consciousness. This can be accomplished in the very first word of the Shema.

Shema (**שמע**) is spelled *shin* (**ש**) *mem* (**מ**) *ayin* (**ע**). The Zohar states that the last letter, the *ayin*, is significant because it has a numerical value of seventy. In general, seventy is seen as representing plurality as it exists in the mundane world. Therefore, the *ayin* represents the seventy different forces of creation. These seventy forces are manifest in the seventy nations and seventy languages, as well as the seventy descendants who accompanied Jacob to Egypt. In listening to the message of unity in the Shema, one brings these seventy forces into the ear and mind, and unifies them with the Divine.

The Shema can be understood on many levels. However, as a meditation, the main thing is to allow the simple meaning of each word to penetrate the mind. One must understand the words, not with the intellect, but with the soul.

14·The Ladder

One of the most vivid scenes in the Torah is that of Jacob's dream, in which he saw "a ladder standing on earth, with its top reaching heaven" (Gen. 28:12). There is a *midrash* that teaches that this ladder had four steps. According to the great Jewish mystics, they represent the fours steps one must climb to reach the highest level of the spiritual domain.

It is taught that these four steps represent the four levels of meditational involvement: action, speech, thought, and the level above thought. As we have discussed, the level above thought is experienced as nothingness.

These four levels also parallel the four letters of the Tetragrammaton, YHVH(ה ו ה י)(see chapter 7).

The first level is that of action, where we are still involved with our body. This parallels the final *heh*(ה) of the Tetragrammaton, which is the hand that receives. It is through the body that we receive all blessing from God. The "hand" that God gives us to receive His energy is the body, which He created in the Divine image. So the first and lowest level is involvement with the body and action.

The second level is that of speech. On the level of speech, we can be aware that we are communicating with the Divine. Speech is the angelic power in man, through which we can transcend our animal nature. Moreover, speech bridges the gap between the physical and the spiritual, and between man and God. Therefore, the level of speech parallels the *vav* (ו) of the Tetragrammaton, which is the arm with which God reaches out to us. *Vav* has the connotation of connection, and this parallels speech, which connects God and man.

The third level is that of thought. It is through the power of thought that we grasp what we can of the Divine. Thought therefore parallels the first *heh* (ה) of the Divine Name, which is God's "hand that holds." Thought is the "hand that holds" every experience of the Divine that we can experience.

Finally, there is the level above thought, which is experienced as nothingness. This is the ineffable experience of the Divine itself. This is the experience that we have only when all thought is turned off and we enter into the realm of pure experience, which is beyond thought.

The Kabbalists teach that the morning *shacharith* service is divided according to these four steps. The four divisions of the morning service are:

1. The Introductory Readings
2. The Verses of Praise
3. The Shema and its blessings
4. The Amidah

We have discussed the Shema and the Amidah in earlier chapters. Let us now see how they fit into the context of the rest of the service.

The Introductory Readings begin with blessings in which we thank God for our physical nature. They include thanksgiving blessings for our body functions, for our ability to stand, walk, and function in the physical world.

As discussed earlier, the word "blessed" when applied to God denotes His immanence in the world. When we recite the blessings for bodily functions, we are sensitizing ourselves to the Divine that is immanent in our own bodies. Thus, although on this level we may not yet be in touch with our spiritual nature, we become aware of our body as a receptacle for the spiritual. This is the level of the "hand that receives," discussed earlier.

The second half of the introductory section consists of readings dealing with the sacrificial system. These sacrifices consisted of both plants and animals. To understand the significance of these readings in the service, one must understand the place that sacrifice had in ancient Israel. The Hebrew word for sacrifice is *korban,* which literally means "that which is brought close." The animal sacrifices were thus seen as a means of drawing close to God.

The Talmud teaches that man is half animal and half angel. The body is the seat of man's animal nature, while the soul is the seat of his angelic nature. Since the body is the vessel of the soul, man's animal nature is the receptacle for his angelic nature.

There are times when man must elevate his animal nature and use it as a means of serving God. The Torah thus says, "You shall love God your Lord with all your heart and with all your soul" (Deut. 6:5). The Talmud interprets "your heart" to denote man's animal nature and "your soul" to denote his angelic nature. The verse therefore teaches that both must be devoted to the love of God.

When sacrifice was offered in ancient times, it was burned on the Great Altar in the Holy Temple in Jerusalem. The sacrifice symbolized that the animal in man also has a place in serving God. Since it is the body that is the receptacle of the Divine, the body and animal nature must also be "brought close" to God.

Therefore, the Sacrificial Readings in the Introductory Readings serve to make us aware that our bodies are vessels for the Divine. At this point in the service, we are still concerned with action and the physical body, but we are beginning to connect it with the spiritual.

The second part of the service is known as the Verses of Praise, and it consists of Psalms and other biblical praises of God. This part of the service parallels the level of speech. In reciting these biblical verses, we are using speech to connect ourselves to God. In this part of the service, we should also make ourselves keenly aware of the process through which we speak and pronounce the words. We should concentrate on our tongue and lips, and feel how they articulate each sound. This in itself can be a contemplation. We should also carefully listen to each sound and each word as we speak these praises of God.

This section is known in Hebrew as *pesukey de-zimra*, literally, "verses of *zimra*." The Hebrew word *zimra* has a double meaning: it can mean praise, but it also has the connotation of cutting. The Kabbalists therefore note that the verses of *zimra* serve to help us cut ourselves away from the physical. If man is half animal and half angel, then speech is uniquely associated with the angelic side of man. Indeed, where the Torah says, "God formed man from the dust of the earth, and blew in his nostrils a breath of life so that man became a living soul" (Gen. 2:7), the Targum (the authorized Aramaic translation) translates "living soul" as "speaking soul." Man's ability to speak is closely associated with his spiritual nature.

Therefore, during this second part of the service, we become aware of our own spirituality and the connection that we have with God. The praise we chant brings us into the space of this connection, where we can transcend our physical nature. All that exists for us is our speaking to God. The Jewish mystics therefore say that one is in the "World of Speech," since in this state, speech is one's entire world.

Thus, there is an important transition in the first two sections of the service. In the Introductory Readings, we are hovering over the physical world but still attached to it. In the Verses of Praise, we begin to transcend it.

The Verses of Praise conclude with the Song of the Red Sea (Exod. 15). After the Exodus from Egypt, the Israelites were pursued by the Egyptians. God rescued them by splitting the Red Sea and allowing them to cross. The Egyptians who chased them into the sea were drowned when the sea returned to normal. It was only after the crossing of the Red Sea that the Israelites gained total freedom.

The Kabbalists teach that the Egyptian Exile represents states of immature or constricted consciousness (*mochin de-katnuth*). At the end of the Verses of Praise we emerge from constricted consciousness to a state of expanded consciousness (*mochin de-gadluth*). This transition is made when we repeat the Song of the Red Sea.

After having completed the Verses of Praise, we are then ready to begin the third part of the service, which consists of the Shema and its blessings. This section of the service is said to correspond to the "World of Thought." The spiritual ascent that we make here is in pure thought. In the Verses of Praise, thought was secondary to speech; in the Shema and its blessings, speech is secondary to thought. Here, we are in a state of expanded consciousness, where thought is our entire world. The culmination of this section is the Shema itself, where all thought is filled with God's unity.

These first three sections of the service are also said to parallel the three lowest levels of the soul. In Hebrew, the lowest level of the soul is known as *nefesh*, the next is called *ruach*, and the highest is *neshamah*. The word *nefesh* comes from a root denoting "rest," and *ruach* means "wind," while *neshamah* is associated with breath.

The Kabbalists explain the significance of these three levels using a glassblower as an analogy. In this case, the glassblower is the Divine, while the vessel is the person. The glassblowing process begins with the blower's breath (*neshimah*) blowing into the tube that connects his mouth to the vessel he is blowing. This breath then travels through the glassblowing tube as a wind (*ruach*) until it reaches the vessel. Finally, the breath enters the vessel and forms it according to the blower's plan, and there it comes to rest (*nafash*).

In the case of the soul, the "blower" is the Divine. In describing the creation of man, the Torah thus says, "God formed man out of the dust of the earth, and He blew in his nostrils a soul [*neshamah*] of life" (Gen. 2:7). The highest level of the soul is thus the *neshamah*, which is, as it were, the "breath of God." This is the "vessel" that holds the spiritual nature that God wishes to give us. Hence, it can be said to parallel the "hand that gives," the first *heh* of the Tetragrammaton.

The second level is *ruach*, which is the "wind" blowing down to us from God's breath. This "wind" is seen as the connection between God's "mouth," as it were, and the person. Therefore, it parallels the *vav* of the Tetragrammaton and the angelic world, which also denote transition. It is significant that *ruach* is always associated with the spiritual experience, and the expression "Holy Spirit" (*ruach ha-kodesh*) is virtually synonymous with prophecy.

Finally, there is the level of *nefesh*, the lowest level of the soul, where it interfaces with the physical. This is the level where we are able to *accept* the spirituality that God desires to give us. Hence, it parallels the "hand that receives," the final *heh* of the Tetragrammaton. Since this part of the soul is essentially passive rather than active, it is called *nefesh*, which literally means the "resting soul." When the Torah speaks of punishment for certain serious sins, it says, "that soul [*nefesh*] shall be cut off." It speaks of the level of *nefesh*, the level of the soul through which one is able to receive spiritual sustenance from God. When this is cut off from *ruach*, a person is cut off from his spiritual source.

These three levels of the soul represent three levels of inner space. One travels through these three levels in the first three parts of the morning service. In the Introductory Readings, we gain an awareness of *nefesh*, the part of the soul that interfaces with the body. This is the level of action where the person gains an awareness of the body as a receptacle for the spiritual. On this level, one cannot feel the spiritual, but knows that the body is intimately attached to it.

In the Verses of Praise, a person becomes aware of the level of *ruach*, the divine wind-spirit. This is the inner space where one is totally aware of one's own spiritual nature and connection to God. This is also the level of speech. Just as speech traverses distance, so does wind. When you say the words of this section, try to feel the divine "wind" blowing through your being.

It is no accident that the word *ruach* means both "wind" and "spirit." We live in a sea of air that is so familiar to us that we remain totally oblivious to it. Similarly, we are oblivious to the sea of spirituality that surrounds us at all times. Nevertheless, when the air displays energy and moves, we feel it as a wind (*ruach*); when the spiritual displays energy and moves, we have an experience of spirit (*ruach*). The second section of the service is meant to elicit this experience.

In the third part of the service, which consists of the Shema and its blessings, we reach up to the World of Love and the realm of unity. Here, one is aware of *neshamah*, the Breath of God. There is a vast difference between the inner space feeling of *ruach* and that of *neshamah*. It is the difference between feeling a wind and a breath. A wind has energy and force, but it is impersonal. A breath is both personal and intimate. Feeling the breath of one's beloved is a most sensual experience.

Therefore, in the third section of the service, a person has a *neshamah* experience, in which he feels an intimacy with God, as if God were breathing on him, as it were. This is the level of divine love and unity.

After the Shema, one again recounts the story of the Exodus and repeats certain key phrases from the Song at the Sea. This is also a transition, but to a new, even more expanded level of consciousness that will lead to the Amidah. The third part of the service concludes with the blessing "Blessed are You, Adonoy, Redeemer of Israel." The "Israel" in the worshiper is here "redeemed" and allowed to enter the inner reaches of the divine realm.

This is attained in the fourth part of the service, the Amidah. Here, one enters into a realm that transcends thought. In the Amidah, we do not think about the words we are saying, but experience them. This does not mean that we are not aware of the words. Quite to the contrary: we are extremely aware, but on a level that goes beyond thought and penetrates every fiber of our being. It is as if the words are filling our entire consciousness and their innermost meaning is becoming one with the deepest reaches of our souls.

This level parallels the *yod* of the Tetragrammaton. This is not the level of the "hand" or "mind" that holds the divine essence, but the essence itself. Therefore, on this level, one is intimately aware of the essence in each word.

This level corresponds to a still higher level of the soul, even above *neshamah*. This fourth level of the soul is known as *chayyah*, which literally means "life force." If the level of *neshamah* involves an awareness of the breath of the Divine, then the level of *chayyah* is the awareness of the divine life force itself.

The Zohar states that a kiss is the merging of one breath with another. Love begins with physical attraction. Then, as lovers begin communication, they begin to speak. As they get closer, they stop speaking and are merely aware of each other's breath. Finally, they come still closer, and their communication becomes a kiss, at which point they are actually in physical contact. At this moment, in the kiss, they are aware of each other's life force. Kissing is thus a natural consequence of increased intimacy in speech. The two mouths come closer and closer and progress from speech, to breath, to the kiss. Thus, there are four levels in the intimacy of love: physical attraction, speech, breath, and the kiss. These same levels exist in the relationship of a person with the Divine.

The service is designed to bring a person through these four levels. In the Introductory Readings, one is attracted to God with one's physical being. In the Verses of Praise, one communicates with the Divine in speech. In the Shema and its blessings, one experiences intimacy with the Divine on the level of breath. Finally, the Amidah is the kiss, and the level of communication is with the life force itself. It is significant that the level of communication of the Amidah is life force, since the Hebrew word for "life" is *chai* (חי), which has a numerical value of eighteen (8 + 10). Eighteen is also the basic number of blessings in the Amidah.

After the Amidah, there is a fifth section of the service, which is known as the "Descent of Influx" (*yeridath ha-shefa*). Here one strives to bring the spiritual levels that one has attained during the service into one's life. It is not enough to have the experience; one must also be able to hold on to it and keep it for the entire day.

We thus see that the daily service is much more than a mere

"order of prayer." It is, in fact, a spiritual pilgrimage in which one rises from one level of spirituality to the next, gaining ever-increasing intimacy with the Divine. It is a daily meditation experience that can have the most profound spiritual effects on a person.

15 · In All Your Ways

One of the key teachings of Judaism is that one can experience a closeness to God in anything one does. The Talmud bases this teaching on the verse "In all your ways know him" (Prov. 3:6) and says that this short verse "contains the entire essence of the Torah." It teaches that no matter what a person does, he can dedicate it to God and make it into an act of worship. Even the most mundane act can serve as a link to the Divine.

Take a routine task, something that has to be done, like washing the dishes. It can be pure drudgery; however, if one elevates it to an act of worship, it can be an exalting experience through which one draws close to God. It all depends on one's intentions.

When washing dishes, one can think about the fact that the dishes will be clean for the next meal. The meal will be eaten so that the family will have the strength to go through another day, and perhaps gain a new and deeper awareness of God. People will recite blessings over food, making the act of eating into a sacrament. Thus, the washing of dishes, at least indirectly, can be seen as a means through which one will draw close to God in other ways.

The act itself can also be an elevating experience. Imagine that you are about to prepare a meal for the person you love more than anyone else in the world. Imagine that it is not just an ordinary meal, but one to celebrate an important milestone in your lives. All the love that you feel for this person is going into the preparation of this meal. It is to be a special meal, with everything just perfect.

Now imagine that you are washing the dishes that are going to be used for this meal. You would want every dish to be perfectly clean and shiny, without the slightest speck or spot. The act of washing dishes would then also be an act of love.

Think for a moment of the greatest love you ever had in your life. If you have ever been deeply in love, you know that there is a stage where the mind becomes almost obsessed with the one you love. No matter what you are doing—eating, sleeping, working—the person you love hovers at the edge of your consciousness. Everything else is unimportant—it is as if you are just marking time until you can see or speak to this person again. All other pleasures in the world are secondary to the pleasure of being in this person's presence.

It is possible to love God in this manner, and with even greater intensity. There is a level of love at which one constantly yearns and longs for a closeness to God. No matter what pleasures one enjoys, they are nothing compared with this feeling of closeness. True love for God can surpass even the greatest passion that can exist between man and woman.

When a person has such a love for God, then even an act as mundane as washing dishes becomes an expression of this love. Then, the more one concentrates on the act of washing a dish, the greater and more intense this love becomes. The act itself becomes an expression of love.

The more aware we become of God's love for us, the more open we become to loving God. If we concentrate on what we are doing, even an act as lowly as washing a dish can connect us to God. We may say to ourselves: Now I am washing a dish because I will be sharing a meal with God, and I love God more than anything else in the world.

Even a mundane act can thus become a vehicle to connect God's love for us to our love for Him. It is as if God's love is on one side, our love is on the other, and the act is in the middle.

This is reminiscent of our discussion of the Shema (see chapter

13). As noted there, the prayer right before the Shema ends with a statement of God's love for Israel; after the Shema, we say, "You shall love God, your Lord, with all your heart. . . ." We saw how the Shema, as the expression of God's unity, bridged these two loves. Therefore, when a person wishes to make an action represent the connection between the two loves, the action itself must be an expression of God's unity. This can be understood in the following manner:

If God is One, then He and His will must also be One. Since God is absolutely One, then He must be identical with His will.

On the other hand, things exist only because God wills them to exist. If God did not will an object to exist, it would simply stop existing. God gave each thing existence through His will, and it is only through His will that it can continue to exist.

This implies that God's will is in everything. However, if God is identical with His will, then God must also be in everything. Therefore, every action and every thing must be permeated with God's essence.

Now imagine that you are washing the dishes. You are concentrating on the act of washing, clearing the mind of all other thoughts. Any other thought that enters the mind is gently pushed aside, so that the task at hand totally fills the mind. You are totally aware of the act you are doing, and as far as you are concerned, nothing else exists in the universe.

Concentrate for a moment on a dish and realize that it is an expression of God's will and essence. Although it may be hidden, there is a spark of the Divine in the dish. There is also a spark of the Divine in the water with which you are washing the dish. When a person develops such an awareness, then even the most mundane act can become an intimate experience of the Divine.

This concept is manifestly more explicit in Jewish teachings regarding eating. It is taught that when a person eats, he should concentrate totally on the food and the experience of eating it, clearing the mind of all other thoughts. He should have in mind that the taste of the food is also an expression of the Divine in the food, and that by eating it, he is incorporating this spark of the Divine into his body. A person can also have in mind that he will dedicate the energy that he will obtain from this food to God's service. It is taught that when a person does this, it is counted as if the food he is eating is a sacrifice on the Great Altar in Jerusalem.

Therefore, eating itself can be a form of meditation as well as a means through which one can draw closer to God. It is for this reason that it was ordained that a blessing be recited before one begins eating. The blessing varies with each food, and a complete list can be found in most standard prayer books. Each general category of food has its own blessing. Thus, for example, the blessing over food that grows on a tree is:

Barukh Attah Adonoy, Elohenu Melekh ha-Olam,
   Borey peri ha-etz.
Blessed are You, O God, our Lord, King of the Universe,
   Who creates the fruit of the tree.

The first thing that one notices is that the blessing is in the present tense rather than in the past. The wording is, "Who *creates* the fruit," and not, "Who *created*." The blessing therefore immediately indicates that God's creative power is in the fruit right now, at the instant one is eating it. As soon as one has this awareness, the act of eating becomes an act of communing with the Divine.

I have already discussed the significance of the word "blessed" as it applies to God. Therefore, when we open the blessing with the words "Blessed are You . . . ," we are expressing our realization that God is immanent in all creation. When the blessing is said with deep concentration, as in the Amidah, the words themselves make us aware of this immanence.

Right after that, we refer to God as "our Lord" (*Elohenu*). As discussed before, this indicates that He makes Himself available to us and allows us to experience Him. It is because of God's immanence that He is accessible to us, and we can experience His closeness whenever we make a sincere attempt to do so.

Too much emphasis on God's immanence, however, might lead a person to minimize His greatness. One might even get too familiar with the Divine. Therefore, the very next expression in the blessing is "King of the Universe." We make ourselves aware that this Presence that we are addressing is the same Infinite Being that rules all creation, the same Presence that exists throughout the entire universe, in stars and galaxies beyond comprehension.

When we say that God is "King of the Universe," we avoid falling into the intellectual trap of pantheism. We are aware that God's presence permeates all things, but we realize that this does not mean that God is no more than the sum of all things. We therefore say that God is King of the Universe. A king's power may fill his entire kingdom, but this does not mean that the king and his kingdom are one and the same. Although God's essence permeates all creation, God Himself is infinitely higher than anything and everything He created.

We then conclude the blessing in the appropriate manner. In our example, the conclusion is, "Who creates the fruit of the tree." Other endings are, "Who creates the fruit of the ground," for most vegetables; "Who created the fruit of the vine," for wine; "Who brings forth bread from the earth," for bread; "Who creates various nourishing foods," for grain products; and "by Whose word all things exist," for any food not in one of the above categories. We designate the food and make ourselves aware of God's creative power and immanence in the food we eat.

The blessing should be said very slowly, with the mind cleared of all extraneous thought. When said in such a manner, the blessing before food can be a very powerful meditation.

People sometimes ask why Judaism does not have an eating discipline like many of the Eastern religions. Of course, Judaism does have one important eating discipline, namely keeping kosher. An animal must be slaughtered in a very specific manner before it can be eaten, and all the blood must be drained out completely. Certain species are absolutely forbidden.

The most important discipline of Judaism, however, involves the blessing. When a blessing is recited before eating, then the act itself becomes a spiritual undertaking. Through the blessing, the act of eating becomes a contemplative exercise. Just as one can contemplate a flower or a melody, one can contemplate the act of eating. One opens one's mind completely to the experience of masticating the food and fills the awareness with the taste and texture of the food. One then eats very slowly, aware of every nuance of taste.

When one eats with the proper state of consciousness, one can make do with a much smaller amount of food. The body's own wisdom determines how much food is required, and no more is desired, since one does not eat out of compulsion or out of nervous habit. Therefore, one eats exactly as much as one requires, no more and no less.

In general, then, Judaism sees even the most mundane acts as means of gaining God consciousness. Working, eating, dressing, all can be made into acts of worship. A person who does this can begin to see God in every facet of life.

16·The Commandments

In the previous chapter, I discussed how even mundane acts can be made into an act of worship through which one can experience the Divine. There are other actions, however, that are specifically designed to bring a person closer to God. These include the many commandments and rituals of Judaism.

It is taught that the Torah contains a total of 613 commandments. The idea of keeping 613 commandments may seem overwhelming. Indeed, one must be a scholar to even be able to find all 613 commandments in the Torah. However, there are a number of published lists of the commandments, and a study of these lists will show that most of the commandments pertain only to special cases, special people, or special places. Thus, for example, a large number of the commandments deal with the service in the Holy Temple in Jerusalem, which no longer exists, and even when it did exist, many of the rituals were the responsibility only of the *kohen* priests. Other commandments involve agriculture or criminal law and have little bearing on the day-to-day practice of Judaism.

Therefore, if one studies the commandments, it turns out that, for the most part, the practice of Judaism is defined by three or four dozen of them. These commandments define the structure of Judaism, and keeping them is what makes a person an observant Jew.

Besides the commandments found in the Torah itself, there are numerous rituals and customs that have become an integral part of Judaism. A number of these were legislated by the ancient sages because they saw that an additional spiritual aïd or dimension was needed by the Jewish people. The additional rituals provided this dimension and allowed the person to have a full spiritual life, even where it was impossible to keep all the commandments.

Thus, for example, the Torah prescribes that all Jewish holidays be observed for one day. Later, when there was trouble fixing the calendar, it was legislated that festivals be kept for two days outside the Holy Land. On the surface, the reason was that there was a question as to which day the festival fell on. The Zohar, however, states that outside the Holy Land, it was impossible to accomplish spiritually in one day what must be accomplished on a festival. Therefore, a second day was added so that one would be able to complete the spiritual growth implied by the festival.

The same, to a large degree, is true of customs. The Talmud states that when the Jewish people adopt a custom, they are doing so on the basis of what is very close to prophetic inspiration. Witnessing the establishment of a custom, Hillel (first century B.C.E.) remarked, "Let the Israelites follow their own course. If they are not prophets, then they are apprentice prophets." This suggests that people have the power, collectively, to feel a spiritual need and fill it. Therefore, even customs can contain a powerful degree of spiritual energy.

It was also decreed that before performing many commandments and rituals, a blessing must be said. As discussed earlier, every blessing is a statement of God's immanence. However, since a commandment comes from God, it is also an expression of His will. As we have discussed earlier, God is identical with His will (at least on one level of understanding), and therefore God is uniquely present in His commandments. When a person performs a ritual mandated by a commandment, he or she has the opportunity to create a unique bond with God.

All the blessings said over commandments have a common beginning:

Barukh Attah Adonoy, Elohenu Melekh ha-Olam
  asher kideshanu be-mitzvotav, ve-tzivanu . . .
Blessed are You, O God, our Lord, King of the Universe,
  Who sanctified us with His precepts, and commanded
  us . . .

In the blessing, we state that God "sanctified us with His commandments." In this statement, we recognize the commandments as a means through which God sanctifies our lives and raises us above the mundane. We see that the commandments are a special means that God gave us to experience the Divine. When keeping any ritual, we should see it as an expression of our desire to be close to God. Here again, love provides a pertinent example.

Imagine that you are in love. You are constantly trying to do things to please your beloved and draw closer to him or her. If the beloved makes a request, you may see it as a unique opportunity to express your love. There is no greater pleasure than doing something like that; the very fact that you are doing something that your beloved desires makes it a total act of love.

The same is true of God's commandments. These are not acts that one does on one's own to express one's love for God, but acts that God has asked us to do as an expression of this love. If one keeps God in mind when observing a commandment, the experience can be one of overwhelming love for and closeness to the Divine.

Furthermore, since these are God's commandments, they are closely and uniquely linked to God's will. This expression of the divine will is every bit as real as the will through which God created the universe. Therefore, a commandment is every bit as real as a physical object. If one meditates on this, one can see the observance as something real and palpable, filled with the Divine.

When you keep a commandment, try meditating on the fact that God's will is in the commandment. In a deep meditative state, you will actually be able to feel God's will in the action and the fact that God and His will are One.

Besides the blessing said before a commandment, there is another meditation that is recommended by the great Jewish mystics. It says:

I am doing this for the sake of the unification of the Holy One, blessed be He and His Divine Presence, with awe and love, in the name of all Israel.

The term "Holy One, Blessed be He" (*Kudesha berikh Hu*) is a common Aramaic term used to denote God, found in both the Talmud and the Zohar. To understand the meaning of this meditation, we must understand why this particular term is used.

I have explained that the word "blessed" when applied to God refers to His immanence. However, we must also understand what the word "holy" means when applied to God. Usually, when we say that something is holy, we mean that it is close to God or pertains to His worship. But what does the word mean when applied to God Himself?

When we use the word "holy" to describe a person or object, we are indicating not only that it is dedicated to God, but also that it is both separated and distinguished from the mundane. Therefore, when we say that God is "holy," we are saying that He is separated from the mundane to the greatest extent imaginable. Therefore, when we say that God is "holy," we are saying that He is utterly transcendent.

In Judaism, there is always a tension between God's immanence and His transcendence. When we say that God is "blessed" we recognize that He is holy, while when we say that He is "holy" we are aware that He is transcendent. God is, as it were, both very near and very far. The Kabbalists express it by saying that God both fills all creation and surrounds all creation. On the other hand, He is immanent and fills all creation; "no place is devoid of Him." On the other hand, He surrounds all creation and is totally Other than it.

When we speak of God as "the Holy One, blessed be He," we

are saying that He is "the transcendent One, Who is immanent." We are declaring that God is utterly transcendent, but that we can also experience Him as being immanent. The term "Holy One, blessed be He" therefore bridges the gap between God's transcendence and His immanence. It is as if God was very far away but was stretching out His hand to enable us to grasp it. This is represented by the *vav* (ו) of the Tetragrammaton, as I have discussed earlier. Indeed, the Kabbalists explicitly state that the expression "Holy One, blessed be He" denotes the Divine on the level of this *vav*.

Furthermore, the Zohar states that "the Holy One, blessed be He, and the Torah are One." This is because the Torah is the means through which God reaches out to us from His transcendence. Indeed, the Torah uses anthropomorphisms to describe God primarily to make Him more understandable and "human" to us and allow us to experience His immanence. The commandments in the Torah also serve as a link between God and human beings.

The Kabbalistic meditation unifies "the Holy One, blessed be He, with His Divine Presence." The Hebrew word for the Divine Presence is *Shekhinah*, which literally means "that which dwells." The *Shekhinah* is a very important concept in Judaism in general.

The *Shekhinah* is said to be wherever God's presence is manifest. Thus, it is taught that the *Shekhinah* was on Mount Sinai when God gave the commandments and later in the Holy Temple in Jerusalem. Furthermore, when an individual experienced prophecy, it was said that the *Shekhinah* rested on him. Since the word *Shekhinah* comes from the root *shakhan*, meaning "to dwell," *Shekhinah* denotes that God appears to be "dwelling" in a certain place.

But what does it mean when we say that God "dwells" in a place? It cannot be taken literally, since God's essence fills all creation. When we say that God "dwells" in a certain place, we really mean that people can have an additional awareness of God there. Wherever the *Shekhinah* rests, there is an enhanced ability to experience the Divine.

When God allows His *Shekhinah* to rest in a certain place or situation, it is as if He were giving us a hand with which to receive the experience of the Divine.

This is represented by the last *heh* (ה) of the Tetragrammaton. Here again, the Kabbalists teach that the *Shekhinah* represents the same level of the Divine as this final *heh*.

Therefore, when this meditation speaks of uniting "the Holy One, blessed be He, and His *Shekhinah*," it is speaking of uniting the levels of the *vav* and the *heh:* the arm reaching out to us, and the hand that God gives us so that we may receive. Indeed, some versions of this meditation state explicitly that the *vav* and the *heh* are being united. Observing a commandment allows us to unite the male and female aspects of God's presence in the world.

This is the essential purpose of keeping a commandment. God is always stretching out His arm to us, willing to give of His essence and spirituality. Before we can take it from Him, we must have a vessel with which to hold it, a "hand" with which to receive. The way we do this is by making ourselves receptacles for the Divine. God gives us the hand with which to receive the Divine, but we must bring it together with the outstretched arm. The goal of the commandments is to unite the *vav* and the *heh*.

When we say the above meditation, we should bear in mind that we are receptacles for the Divine. Try to feel the great hollow inside yourself that can be filled only by God's essence, and more than anything in the world, yearn that this hollow be filled.

At the same time, we should also be aware of God's presence all around us. We should contemplate the fact that God always wants to make Himself available, but needs an act on our part. The commandments serve as this medium, and through them God's essence is brought into our being. Therefore, when performing any commandment or ritual, we should be aware that we are drawing into ourselves the light of the Divine.

The meditation goes on to say that the commandment is being done with "love and awe." As we have seen, keeping a commandment can be a powerful expression of love. Love is the feeling that one wishes to unite with the Divine. There must be a boundary on this love, or one can become swallowed up by it completely. Therefore, love for the Divine must be balanced by awe. Love draws us closer to God, but awe keeps us from getting too close.

When we learn to look at the rituals and commandments in this light, all of Judaism takes on new significance. We can see the commandments as the path that God Himself gave for us to come close to Him and experience His presence.

17 · Between Man and Woman

In earlier chapters, I discussed how the last two letters of the Tetragrammaton, *vav* (ו) and *heh* (ה), represent the male and female forces of providence. The male force is that which acts upon the world, while the female force is that which allows the world to be receptive to God's power.

This is one reason that we refer to God in the male gender when we pray. Of course, although we usually refer to God as a male, in His true essence He is without gender. We refer to Him as a male, however, because we want Him to act upon the world through the male force of providence. We then leave ourselves open to God's providence, as a female is open to her mate.

The expression "the Holy One, blessed be He" is in the male gender and is therefore seen as denoting the male force of providence. It also relates to the *vav* of the Tetragrammaton.

The Hebrew word for "Divine Presence," on the other hand, is *Shekhinah*, which is a feminine noun. The *Shekhinah* denotes the final *heh* in the divine name as well as the female power of providence.

It is significant that the Torah presents man and woman together as comprising the image of the Divine. The Torah thus says, "God created man in His image, in the image of God He created him, male and female He created them" (Gen. 1:27). This clearly implies that male and female together form the "image of God."

The reason for this is obvious. A male and female have the power to do the most Godlike thing possible, namely, to create life. The power to conceive a child is so Godlike that the Talmud states that when man and woman create a child, God Himself is their third partner.

Therefore, a husband and wife should see each other as being a reflection of the Divine. When a woman looks at her husband, she should see him as a reflection of "the Holy One, blessed be He," the male aspect of the Divine. Similarly, when a husband looks at his wife, he should see her as the Divine Presence (*Shekhinah*), the feminine aspect of the Divine.

When a person attains this goal, he will fully appreciate his wife's beauty and see it as a reflection of the Divine. He will then also be aware of her inner beauty, which is a reflection of the beauty of the *Shekhinah*. When one can contemplate this, one is filled with a love toward one's spouse that parallels the supernal love between the masculine and feminine forces of the Divine.

The Torah tells about the love between Jacob and Rachel, and describes it as one of the greatest loves the world has ever seen. It tells how Jacob was willing to work as an indentured servant for seven years to win Rachel's hand, and how the seven years "passed like days, so much did he love her" (Gen. 29:20). The Jewish mystics explain that Jacob saw himself as the male aspect of the Divine and Rachel as the female aspect; he therefore had a love that was a counterpart of the love on high.

When one is looking for a spiritual master, the first thing to examine is the master's relationship with his wife. From the way a man treats his wife, one can know how he relates to the *Shekhinah*. No matter how deep the master's meditations seem to be, no matter how wise his words, if he does not have a good relationship with his wife, then there is something missing from his spirituality. Conversely, when a man has a good relationship with his wife, even in the face of temptation and adversity, it is a clear indication that he is on a high spiritual level.

I once knew a member of the Musar school of meditation who was married to a woman with a severe mental illness. But whereas she was filled with anger and abuse, he responded with love and devotion. No matter how mean she was to him, he constantly saw her as his link with the Divine, and gave love and respect accordingly. It would be nice to say that this love cured her, but in actuality it did not. However, when he was left a widower as an old man, this man would constantly say how much he appreciated and missed his wife.

It is also significant that there is no encouragement of celibacy in the Jewish tradition, mystical or otherwise. Moses, the greatest of all mystics and prophets, was married, as were all the prophets and sages. Sex is seen not as a weakness of the flesh or as a necessary evil, but as a means to drawing close to God on a most intimate level.

When man and wife see each other as personifications of the divine image, then the sexual act becomes something holy. It is nothing less than the coming together of the male and female forces of creation. On a physical level, this has the power to create a child, but these forces parallel those on high which brought all creation into existence.

The male and female forces of creation are represented by the *yod* (י) and the *heh* (ה) of the Tetragrammaton. This is very closely related to a fascinating Talmudic teaching: The Hebrew word for man is *iysh* (אִישׁ), while the word for woman is *ishah* (אִשָּׁה). If one looks at the words, one sees that the word *iysh* contains a *yod* (י), while *ishah* contains a *heh* (ה). The Talmud says that these are the *yod* and *heh* of the Tetragrammaton.

If the *yod* and *heh* are removed from *iysh* and *ishah*, then the remaining letters of both words spell out *esh* (אֵשׁ), the Hebrew word for "fire." The fires of passion that unite man and woman are seen as receptacles for the letters of the Divine Name, and hence, for the masculine and feminine elements of the Divine Essence. The passion that draws man and woman together stems from the fact that man and woman are counterparts of the male and female archetypes on high.

Therefore, when husband and wife are intimate, a man can see himself as being filled with the male aspect of the Divine, making an intimate connection with the female aspect. Similarly, a woman can see herself as the female aspect, receiving the male aspect. They can both realize that through their union, they are creating an "image of God."

For this to be accomplished, it is very important to avoid any extraneous thoughts during the sexual act. Partners should not think of any member of the opposite sex other than the sexual partner of the moment. As in any meditation involving action, concentration should be totally on the act itself, with all extraneous thoughts gently pushed aside.

There are several guidelines that are found in the Talmud and Kabbalah to enhance the meditative aspects of the act. First, the experience is meant to be primarily tactile, involving the sense of touch. Therefore, it should be performed in a room as dark as possible. Each party should have nothing distracting him or her from the experience.

It is also taught that there should be no clothing intervening between the two bodies. The Torah speaks of man and woman becoming "one flesh" (Gen. 2:24). This indicates that flesh should be in direct contact with flesh, so that the tactile experience is maximized.

The Kabbalah teaches that the sexual act should begin with words of endearment and then progress to kissing, hugging, and caressing, and finally to total intimacy. It is as if the process begins with the head and mind in speech and kissing. It then is drawn down to the hands and body in hugging and caressing. Finally, it is drawn to the reproductive organs, which are the seat of the greatest sexual pleasure. The sexual energy can be felt traveling down the spine and through the body, leading to the most sensitive areas.

God created the sexual act as one of the greatest pleasures that a human being can experience. For one thing, the act had to be pleasurable so that human beings would be drawn to it and thus perpetuate the species. But on a much deeper level, it is so great a pleasure because it allows man and woman together to emulate the Divine.

When a man and woman experience pleasure from each other, they can contemplate this pleasure as a meditative experience. This will have the immediate effect of enhancing the pleasure manyfold. If they see this pleasure as a gift of God, they will have great joy from it and, at the same time, experience a feeling of thanksgiving. On a deeper level, they can be aware of the spark of the Divine in the pleasure itself and elevate it to its source.

If a couple has such intentions, then the sexual act can be something holy. The Torah says that a married man may not "diminish his wife's conjugal rights" (Exod. 21:10). The Talmud interprets this to mean that it is one of the divine commandments that a husband and wife be intimate at regular intervals. Therefore, when being intimate, a husband and wife can also meditate on the fact that they are fulfilling one of God's commandments. Sex is not simply a mundane act that is being elevated, but a sacred act in its own right.

Very important in making sex a holy act is keeping the rules of family purity. This involves the woman's counting seven days after the end of her period and then immersing in a *mikveh* (ritual bath). The monthly menses are seen as a cleansing process, and immersion in the *mikveh* as a process of rebirth. (The philosophy of the *mikveh* is discussed at length in my book *The Waters of Eden*.) In many ways, immersion in the *mikveh* is more important to making sex a holy act than even marriage itself.

In general, using meditative techniques during intimacy can enhance the pleasure immeasurably. Such a practice focuses the minds of both partners exclusively on their mates and thus serves to strengthen the marriage bond. Couples who regularly use meditative techniques during intimacy have experienced important gains in their feelings toward each other. Couples who were experiencing marital difficulties found that when their sex life was sanctified, their love grew and other problems seemed to become inconsequential.

The type of meditation that a couple can do when they wish to conceive a child is somewhat different. This is because if they are on a certain level of consciousness, the thoughts that they have during intimacy can have a strong effect on the child conceived.

The Torah teaches that when Jacob wanted his sheep to conceive spotted, banded, or striped offspring, he cut rods with the appropriate markings, and set them out where the sheep mated (Gen. 30:37,38). It is taught that Jacob meditated on these rods, and when he was in a very high level of consciousness, he was able to project his thoughts on the the sheep being conceived and thus influence their markings. Deep meditation can have an effect on the genetic structure of one's offspring, as well as the child's spiritual makeup.

Therefore, when a couple wish to conceive, they should decide what traits they would consider most desirable in the child. They should agree on what they consider most important, and what they would most want their child to be. Then, using visualization techniques discussed in chapter 8, they should both visualize the child they want to conceive during intercourse. If this is done with total concentration, it can have a positive influence on the conceived child. While it is not a foolproof technique, especially if the members of the couple are not expert meditators, experience has shown it to have significant influence. Experience has also shown that couples who have difficulty in conceiving often have success when using such an imaging technique.

For many people, sex is associated with guilt and shame. But if we understand that God gave us sexual pleasure as a gift, we will realize that we can enjoy it to the fullest.

Of course, sex is also an area of great temptation. A person may have committed sexual acts, such as adultery, which are regarded as sinful. Here, too, one must realize that sins can be repented; as the Talmud states, "Nothing can stand before repentance." Even if one has fallen into temptation, one can ask, with all one's heart, for God's forgiveness. The fact that a person may have sinned or done wrong need not diminish or destroy his or her ability to experience the Divine.

Judaism views the sexual act as something very holy. It is a means through which a person can experience great intimacy with God. Judaism surrounds the sexual act with many rules and prohibitions, not because it views sex as something dirty or shameful, but because it views sex as something so holy that it must not be misused. Used correctly, with the right intentions and thoughts, sex can be the purest and holiest experience in the world, and meditation can enhance this aspect of the experience.

18 · Remolding the Self

One of the most important meditative movements in Judaism is associated with the Musar school, founded by Rabbi Yisrael Salanter (1810–1883). *Musar*, self-perfection, was always an important element in Judaism; important texts on the subject were published as early as the tenth century. The Musar movement, however, made self-perfection its primary focus. The movement taught that a person should continually strive to grow spiritually, ethically, and morally throughout the course of his lifetime.

Interpersonal relationships were given a high priority in the Musar movement. It was not enough to be able to experience the Divine; one also had to be able to get along with others in the best possible manner. Anger, hatred, revenge, gossip, and jealousy were seen as bad habits that could stunt a person's spiritual growth. The premise was that if we grow in our relationship to God, we should also grow in our ability to relate in a positive way to our fellow human beings. The Musar school thus strove to make every individual into a saint in every sense of the word. People were taught to be sensitive to their own shortcomings and were encouraged to create personal programs to rectify them one by one.

To some extent, the Musar movement was a reaction to the Chasidic movement. Chasidism began as a mystical movement. In order to climb high spiritual mountains, experienced guides, or *rebbes,* were needed. In some Chasidic circles, however, the guide became more important than the mountain. Many Chasidim regarded their *rebbe* as the paradigm of the saintly man and lived the righteous life vicariously through him.

The Musar movement developed among the Mitnaggedim, opponents of the Chasidic movement. Musar schools taught that it was not enough to live the righteous life through a master. Every individual had an obligation to strive to live the righteous life in his own right. Beyond that, the Musar movement offered a program through which every person could gradually perfect himself.

There is an extensive Musar literature in Hebrew. Some of the most important Musar works, such as *Path of the Upright (Mesillath Yesharim),* by Moses Hayim Luzzatto, and *Ways of the Righteous (Orchoth Tzaddikim),* anon., have been translated into English.

The first part of the Musar program was to make a daily habit of reading a lesson from a classical Musar work. After reading the lesson, one was to spend a short period of time contemplating it and relating it to one's own life.

As the individual began to advance, this contemplation became a meditation. One would read a lesson from a classical Musar text on how to improve the ethical, moral, and religious quality of one's life, then meditate on this lesson for twenty to thirty minutes. This is a simple type of meditation, similar to the one described in chapter 3, where I discussed meditating on how to rearrange your life. It is a meditation in which one considers a particular aspect of one's life and thinks about ways to improve it.

In meditations such as these, extraneous thoughts are gently pushed out of the mind. Some authorities, such as the Baal Shem Tov, however, maintained that a person should pay attention to extraneous thoughts, since they could provide clues as to what direction to take. One may wish to make mental notes of these extraneous thoughts and then analyze them to see how to make use of them to help attain one's goals.

The program of self-improvement could include more than just moral issues. The Musar schools saw their method as a way of becoming a more effective human being. Problems such as shyness, indecision, lack of motivation, and the like could also be helped through Musar methods.

The second part of the Musar program consists of a mantralike repetition of the concept one is working on. For example, a person may have a tendency to gossip and want to break this habit. He may realize that gossip is harmful to others and morally wrong, and that it is forbidden by the Torah commandment "Do not go as a talebearer among your people" (Lev. 19:16).

The method of breaking the gossip habit would be to take the biblical verse "Do not go as a talebearer among your people" and repeat it every day for a twenty- to thirty-minute period, like a mantra. As one works on it, the message is gradually absorbed, and the self-control necessary to avoid gossip is attained.

Another effective technique is described by Rabbi Nachman of Bratslav. This technique consists in speaking to various parts of the body. If a person wishes to change a certain trait, he can talk to the part of the body associated with that trait, and in this way change his actions.

Taking the above example of gossip, a person could use Rabbi Nachman's technique and speak to his tongue, telling it never to say anything against another person. If one does this for a fixed amount of time every day, this, too, can be an effective form of meditation.

Let us say that you want to lose weight. You can use Musar and other meditative techniques in various ways. You can simply use the phrase "I am going to lose weight" as a mantra. You can speak to your body and tell it that you want it to be slim. You can also use an imaging technique: imagine yourself slim, what you would look like, and how it would feel to be carrying less weight. Gradually your self-image will start to change. You can speak to your mouth, telling it not to eat so much, and to your stomach, telling it to crave less food. A combination of techniques can be effective even in overcoming lifelong habits.

There are several hints that the Musar schools give to make any self-improvement program more effective. The first is not to try to make too many changes at once. A Talmudic teaching—"If one tries to grasp too much, one grasps nothing"—is taken as a watchword. Better to be successful in making small changes than to fail at making big ones. If one succeeds in making a small change in one's life, it is easy to build on this success.

The important message is that success breeds success and failure breeds failure. People often try to effect a change in their life-style and make the attempt many times, only to meet with failure. This is particularly true of people who have tried to lose weight or give up smoking.

Take as an example the person who resolves to quit smoking. He keeps his resolution for a few weeks, but then feels that he cannot go for the rest of his life without a cigarette and reverts back to his bad habit. He has experienced a failure, which makes stopping all the more difficult the next time around. After a number of such failures, people give up and feel that the habit in question is beyond their control.

The Musar approach would be to give up smoking for a specified period of time, say thirty days. At the end of the thirty-day period, one could begin smoking again. This is the key to success. During this thirty-day period, a person would not have to confront the fact that he will never taste a cigarette again or that he will have to maintain this level of self-control for years to come. The time of abstinence is manageable because it has a limit.

The point of this technique is that at the end of the thirty-day period, a person is free to choose whether or not to begin smoking again. If he resumes smoking, he does not have to feel like a failure. Quite to the contrary: he has been successful in maintaining his thirty-day abstinence and therefore has a success upon which to build. Later, he can stop for another thirty-day period. After doing this a number of times, he may find that the desire to smoke has waned.

Of course, at the end of any of these thirty-day periods, he may decide not to resume smoking. If one thirty-day period was a success, the second thirty-day period will be even easier. By taking one thirty-day period after another, a person can continually weaken the habit until it ceases to exist.

This is particularly true if, during the period of abstinence, one uses the Musar meditational techniques discussed earlier. One can use the expression "I want to stop smoking" as a mantra to help strengthen one's will, so that by the end of the thirty-day period, the desire to smoke will be diminished. Other meditational techniques can also be helpful.

The idea of using thirty-day periods is a very powerful tool in spiritual growth. Many moral or ethical habits are easier to break than smoking or eating habits, since in the latter one must deal with the body as well as the mind. Many bad moral or ethical habits can be overcome in a thirty-day period.

You can work on a relatively large number of character traits over the course of years and thus continually grow, both spiritually and morally. You can in fact remold yourself into the good and righteous person you wish to be. Where you are is not as important as where you are heading. If you are willing to devote your life to continued growth, there are virtually no limits to the levels you can reach.